GW01417549

Pharmacy Or

Sixth edition

Contents

Preface

As I earned my degree in pharmacy, I began to recognize the imminent importance of pharmaceuticals for managing the health and well-being of everyone. After watching the recovery of so many of my patients in my years of practice, I realized that my strategies could be used to help others.

In the United Kingdom, training to become a pharmacist incorporates the learning and demonstration of patient-centred care in an integrated, holistic manner. Pharmacists primarily focus on people's individual health needs, but are also involved in auditing pharmacy services, managing teams and promoting health.

After completing four years of undergraduate studies, and another fifty-two weeks of trainee pharmacist training. Everyone who sits on the exam hopes that after all those years of hard work; they overcome the final hurdle. This book series was designed to assist with exam practice, whilst providing practise of GPhC style clinical and mathematical exam questions, exercises, and case studies. The SPC questions have specifically been formulated to help you to navigate your way around SPCs of various medicinal products to accurately answer exam questions. This book should be used as a revision aid to help increase your efficiency and exam performance.

Every individual sitting the registration exam must remember that they are very intelligent and capable of passing the exam because they have already achieved a master's degree in pharmacy. To get the positive results that candidates deserve, they must commit to being positive. I know that you will be a great and successful pharmacist. Your hard work will pay off to achieve your dream.

All the best

Amit Luthra
The Pharmacy OnBoard team

Abbreviations

AC	Before food
ACBS	Advisory Committee on Borderline Substances, see Borderline Substances
ACE	Angiotensin-converting enzyme
ACEI	Angiotensin-converting enzyme inhibitor
ADHD	Attention deficit hyperactivity disorder
A & E	Accident and Emergency
AED	Anti-epileptic drugs
AF	Atrial fibrillation
AIDS	Acquired immunodeficiency syndrome
ALT	Alternative
AMP	Ampoule
Ante	Before
Applic	Apply
Approx.	Approximately
AUR	Appliance Use Review
AV	Atrioventricular
BAN	British Approved Name
BD	Twice daily
BMI	Body mass index
BNF	British National Formulary
BP	British Pharmacopoeia
BP	Blood pressure
BPM	Beats per minute
BPC	British Pharmaceutical Codex 1973
BRCA	Breast cancer gene
BSA	Body surface area
BTS	British Thoracic Society
cAMP	Cyclic adenosine monophosphate
CCG	Clinical Commissioning Group

CD	Controlled Drug
CD1	Controlled Drug in Schedule 1 of the Misuse of Drugs Regulations 2001
CD2	Controlled Drug in Schedule 2 of the Misuse of Drugs Regulations 2001
CD3	Controlled Drug in Schedule 3 of the Misuse of Drugs Regulations 2001
CD4 I	Controlled Drug in Schedule 4 (Part I) of the Misuse of Drugs Regulations 2001
CD4 II	Controlled Drug in Schedule 4 (Part II) of the Misuse of Drugs Regulations 2001
CD5	Controlled Drug in Schedule 5 of the Misuse of Drugs Regulations 2001
CFC	Chlorofluorocarbon
CHM	Commission on Human Medicines
CHMP	Committee for Medicinal Products for Human Use
CL-	Chloride ions
CNS	central nervous system
COX	Cyclooxygenase
COPD	Chronic obstructive pulmonary disease
CPPE	Centre for pharmacy postgraduate education
CrCl	Creatinine Clearance (mL/minute)
CSM	Committee on Safety of Medicines
CT	Computerized tomography
DMARD	Disease-modifying antirheumatic drug
DOAC	Direct oral anticoagulants
DPF	Dental Practitioners' Formulary
DPP-4	Dipeptidyl-peptidase 4
DT	Drug Tariff price
E/C	Enteric coated
ECG	Electrocardiogram
EEG	Electro-encephalogram
eGFR	Estimated glomerular filtration rate
EHC	Emergency hormonal contraception

ESR	Erythrocyte sedimentation rate
Extemp	Extemporaneously dispensed
FC	Film-coated
FORT	Strong
FSH	Follicle-stimulating hormone
FSRH	Faculty of Sexual and Reproductive Healthcare
FY1	Foundation Year 1
FY2	Foundation Year 2
G	Gram
GFR	Glomerular filtration rate
GIP	Glucose-dependent insulinotropic polypeptide
GLP-1	Glucagon-like peptide-1
GP	General practitioner
GPhC	General Pharmaceutical Council
GR	Gastro-resistant
GSL	General sales list
GTN	Glyceryl trinitrate
GTT	Drops
HbA1C	Glycated haemoglobin
HDL-cholesterol	high-density lipoprotein cholesterol
HIV	Human immunodeficiency virus
HR	Heart Rate
HRS	Hours
HRT	Hormone replacement therapy
IBS	Irritable bowel syndrome
IBW	Ideal Body Weight
ICS	Inhaled corticosteroid
IM	Intramuscular
INF	Infusion
INJ	Injection
IV	Intravenous

INR	International Normalised Ratio
IUD	Intrauterine Device
JCVI	Joint Committee on Vaccination and Immunisation
K+	Potassium ion
KG	Kilogram
LDL-cholesterol	Low-density lipoprotein cholesterol
L	Litre
LFT	Liver function test
LH	Luteinizing hormone
MANE	Morning
MAOI	Monoamine-oxidase inhibitor
Max	Maximum
MCV	mean corpuscular (CELL) volume
MDU	As directed
MDI	Metered dose inhaler
MEP	Medicines, Ethics and practice guide
MHRA	Medicines and Healthcare products Regulatory Agency
MIN	Minute
MITTE	Send
MG	Milligram
ML	Millilitre
MM	Millimetre
mmHG	Millimetre of mercury
MMR	Measles, mumps and rubella
MR	Modified release
MRI	Magnetic resonance imaging
MUR	Medicines use review
NCL	No cautionary label
NHS	National Health Service
NICE	National Institute for Health and Care Excellence

NMS	New Medicines Service
NOCTE	Night
NPF	Nurse Prescribers' Formulary
NRLS	National Reporting and Learning System
NSAID	Non-steroidal anti-inflammatory drug
NSTEMI	Non-ST-segment elevation myocardial infarction
OC	Oral contraception
OCU	Ocular application
OD	Every day
OM	Every morning
ON	Every night
OP	Original pack
ORT	Oral rehydration therapy
OTC	Over the counter
P	Pharmacy (only)
PA	To the affected area
PAST	Paste
PC	After food
PCT	Primary Care Trust
PEG	Percutaneous endoscopic gastrostomy
PGD	Patient Group Direction
PHE	Public Health England
PIL	Patient information leaflet
PMR	Patient medical record
POM	Prescription-only medication
POM-V	Prescription-only medication veterinarian
PPI	Proton pump inhibitor
PR	Per rectum
PRE-REG	Pre-registration pharmacist
PRN	When required
PT	Patient

QD	Four times daily
QDS	To be taken four times daily
QQH	Every fourth hour
QS	Sufficient
Q12H	Every 12 hours
QQ	Every
®	Trademark
rDNA	Ribosomal Deoxyribonucleic acid
RP	Responsible Pharmacist
RX	Prescription
S/C	sugar-coated
SC	Subcutaneous
SCR	Summary care record
SL	Sublingual
SLS	Selected List Scheme
SMC	Scottish Medicines Consortium
SOP	Standard operating procedure
SPC	Summary of Product Characteristics
SPP.	Species
SSRI	Selective serotonin reuptake inhibitor
STAT	Immediately
STEMI	ST-segment elevation myocardial infarction
TCA	Tricyclic antidepressant
TDD	Three times daily
TDS	To be taken three times daily
TPN	Total parenteral nutrition
TRIT	Serial dilution
TSH	Thyroid stimulating hormone
U&E	Urea and electrolytes
UK	United Kingdom
UTI	Urinary Tract Infection

UV	Ultraviolet
VTE	Venous thromboembolism
WFI	Water for injection
WHO	World Health Organization
WSP	White soft paraffin
W/V	Weight in volume
W/W	Weight in weight
YSP	Yellow Soft Paraffin

Introduction

The pharmacist is often the first healthcare professional that patients and the public will have contact with when seeking help. Thus, a pharmacist's role in this sector within the UK and NHS is vital. The responsibility is significantly more than just dispensing. As a pharmacist's role is becoming more and more clinical, this shift in changing roles brings growth and development to pharmacy as a career.

Pharmacists who choose to follow pharmacy as a career, commit to life-long learning. To be able to effectively carry this out, continual professional development fundamentally allows pharmacists to evaluate and assess their current knowledge. Pharmacists' direct patient care services in the community to promote health, wellness, and disease prevention.

Pharmacists are an integral part of the interdisciplinary approach at all levels of care for all healthcare settings, who collaborate with other healthcare workers to improve pharmaceutical care. The adept knowledge that pharmacists have, is required to create, and review comprehensive drug therapy plans for patients, identify, and achieve optimum therapeutic goals and review all prescribed medications before their dispensing and administration to the patient. Pharmacists must remain competent to ensure they safely evaluate the appropriateness of drug therapy (e.g., drug choice, dose, route, frequency, and duration of therapy).

Pass The Pharmacist Registration Exam has been specifically written following the GPhC registration exam framework. This book comprises over 170 ethics, law, best practices, and situational judgement questions. You may refer to reference sources, however, all the questions comprise vital information needed to derive an answer, to enable you to revise for your exam. The book incorporates clinical patient case studies that enable you to revise various areas of pharmacy practice and relate them to real case studies - as you may encounter in the GPhC assessment. All the questions follow the most current treatment guidelines at the time of writing. This volume should be practised under timed conditions. Pharmacy OnBoard has a panel of successful UK registered, practising pharmacists whom each has invaluable experience in the training of pharmacists over the last decade. Each question has been carefully designed to test your knowledge and challenge your potential. Pharmacy OnBoard endeavours to be used as a comprehensive revision aid, by pharmacy students and pharmacists to gain success.

For more updates on the latest events and revision aids from Pharmacy OnBoard, please visit our Instagram portal @pharmacy_onboard.

Feedback

Pharmacy OnBoard works alongside pharmacy students and pre-registration pharmacists in Great Britain. Established in 2014, the association aims to provide compressive preparatory material, and support to assist trainees on their path towards registration.

As part of this supportive and representative role, Pharmacy OnBoard invited feedback following the publication of the highly successful first and second editions of 'Pass the Pharmacist Registration Exam'. As of 1st July 2019, 984 respondents provided excellent feedback, through this Pharmacy OnBoard has been able to collate feedback and present it to the panel of successful UK registered, practising pharmacists. This was then reviewed and categorised into themes. The feedback included several recommendations, all of which were accepted to better the experience for our trainees and have led to improvements in the sixth edition of this series.

Pharmacy OnBoard hopes that this sixth edition is useful for all stakeholders, particularly trainee pharmacists. Should you have any comments, please do not hesitate to contact us.

Exam technique

Over the past few years, Pharmacy OnBoard has been helping trainee pharmacists take the GPhC exam. We have compiled our top eight tips for gaining success with the pharmacist registration assessment.

1.   **To RELAX:** The pass rate varies every year, depending on the performance of students across the board. The pass mark is around 70%. Unnecessary stress and nervousness only lead to added pressure during the exam. Relaxation before the exam is the key to better performance. Try to practice deep breathing to help calm the nerves. Go in with a calm mind and enable better performance. Sleep early the night before and do not have a heavy breakfast before the exam.

2.   **To BELIEVE in yourself:** The registration assessment is not as hard as you think it is. Most of the time, the mock assessment questions/courses are much more complicated than the real GPhC exam. This is only to ensure that you are better prepared for the assessment. So, if you pass the 'Pharmacy OnBoard' questions with a 70% average, then you should expect an 80% average result in the actual exam.

3.   **To REVISE early:** Do not leave the revision before the exam until April/May time. It is important to ensure that towards the second half of the trainee year, you maintain consistency with the level of revision you undertake. Although, it is never too early to start revision. Our experience with trainee pharmacists, suggests that core revision should begin around January (around 6 months before the assessment). Ensure that you are familiar with the structure and layout of SPC, and PIL which will increase your efficiency with extract questions. Resources such as the BNF, MEP, and GPhC guidance documents should be thoroughly dissected and understood to ensure you have a solid grasp of the fundamental knowledge.

4.   **To familiarise with OTC sale restrictions:** Trainee pharmacists working in community pharmacies will have greater exposure to the sale and supply of OTC medicine sale, than those who work in the hospital/GP or industry

sector. So, ensure, that you have some exposure to OTC licensing and sale requirements. Remember, the registration assessment doesn't discriminate between pharmacy sectors and will test your knowledge across the board through patient case scenarios. Spend some time gaining OTC experience.

5. ***To understand pharmaceutical LAW:***
Understanding pharmacy law is not only necessary for passing the registration assessment but is needed beyond that to become a confident and competent pharmacist. It will allow you to get acquainted with all legal proceedings relevant to human and veterinary medicinal manufacturing, packing, distribution, imports, exports, sales, marketing, licensing and registration of the drugs/medicines and associated penalties.

6. ***To practise TIME management:*** Practicing exam technique is the most important thing you can do, to learn how to finish the registration exam on time. The most important part of time management is practice. You should commit to practising full mock exam papers under timed exam conditions. Managing your time in the GPhC assessment will take off so much pressure and will stop you from making silly mistakes in a panic. Remember to break up the time in advance for each question and capitalise on the reading time for case scenarios. If you find you are dwelling on one question for too long, then move to the next question and return to it later.

7. ***To practise CALCULATIONS:*** Our experience with trainee pharmacist exam preparation suggests that consistent maths calculations practice should begin at least 3 months before the exam. Students should aim to carry out at least 4 pharmaceutical calculation questions per day of varying types, every day. This would ensure that at least by the assessment day you would have practised at least 336 different types of pharmaceutical calculation questions. Pharmacy OnBoard provides a vast range of these types of questions, in the calculations section.

8. ***To use many RESOURCES:*** For success in the registration assessment, it is vital that you use reliable sources to revise from. The more resources used, the wider your knowledge base will be for the exam. The team at

Pharmacy OnBoard has designed MCQs which mirror the format of the registration assessment to allow testing and practice for a wide breadth of pharmaceutical content and objectives. This will provide an objective measurement of your current and prospective ability.

Unit Conversions

Some useful values to remember are:

- *10mg in 1ml = 1% w/v or 1gm in 100mls*
- *1mg in 1ml = 0.1% w/v or 1gm in 1000mls (1 Litre)*
- *1mcg in 1ml = 0.0001% w/v or 1gm in 1,00,000mls*
- *1000mls = 1 Litre*
- *1mL = 1 millilitre*
- *1 mol = 1000 millimole*
- *1 millimole = 1,0000 micromole*
- *1 micromole = 1,000 nanomole*
- *1 mol / litre = 1 mmol/ml*
- *1 Mole = Molecular Weight in grams*
- *1 Molar solution = Relative Molecular Mass in grams in 1 Litre of liquid*

Per cent (%) of w/v	Fraction	Decimal	Proportion	Ratio	Parts
50	1/2	0.5	1 in 2	1:1	1 to 1
33.33	1/3	0.333	1 in 3	1:2	1 to 2
25	¼	0.25	1 in 4	1:3	1 to 3
20	1/5	0.2	1 in 5	1:4	1 to 4
16.66	1/6	0.166	1 in 6	1:5	1 to 5
14.285	1/7	0.14285	1 in 7	1:6	1 to 6
12.5	1/8	0.125	1 in 8	1:7	1 to 7
11.11	1/9	0.1111	1 in 9	1:8	1 to 8
10	1/10	0.1	1 in 10	1:9	1 to 9
9.0909	1/11	0.0909	1 in 11	1:10	1 to 10

The Standard International (SI) unit of mass is the kilogram, and the metric unit of mass is the gram.

Unit of mass	Abbreviation	Equivalent to:
1 Kilogram	Kg	1000 grams
1 Gram	g	1000 milligrams
1 Milligram	mg	1000 micrograms
1 Microgram	mcg	1000 nanograms

The litre is both the SI unit and metric unit of volume. The most used units of volume are litres (L) and millilitres (mL).

Unit of volume	Abbreviation	Equivalent to:
1 Litre	L	1000 millilitres
1 Millilitre	mL	1000 microlitres

Duration of Supply
- 1/7 = 1 day
- 3/7 = 3 days
- 7/7 = 1 week
- 1/52 = 1 week
- 4/52 = 4 weeks
- 1/12 = 1 month

Frequency of Administration
- OD = Once daily
- BD = Twice daily
- TDS = Three times daily
- QDS = Four times daily
- STAT = Immediately

Schedule 1 Controlled Drug POM
Require a licence from the home office to be prescribed (usually hallucinogenic)

Schedule 2 Controlled Drug POM
Healthcare professionals (such as pharmacists) named in the Misuse of Drugs Regulations 2001 have general authority to possess, supply and procure them when acting within capacity. Require safe custody. The Receiving and supplying of these must be recorded in the CD register.

Schedule 3 Controlled Drug POM (No register entry required)
These drugs have a lower tendency to be misused, if misused they are less likely to cause as much harm as schedule 2 controlled drugs
- The balance of stock does not need to be recorded in the CD register

- CD prescription requirements under the Misuse of Drugs Regulations 2001 still apply
- The prescriber must be from the UK
- Emergency supply only allowed for phenobarbital (up to 5 days)
- License is required for import and export

Schedule 4 CD (part 1 benzodiazepines) POM

CD prescription writing requirements as stated in the Misuse of Drugs Regulations 2001 do not apply. The prescriber does not have to be from the UK. This class consists of benzodiazepines, Z drug hypnotics and Sativex.

Schedule 4 CD (part 2 anabolic steroids) POM

CD prescription writing requirements as stated in the Misuse of Drugs Regulations 2001 do not apply. The prescriber does not have to be from the UK. This class consists of anabolic/androgenic steroids/growth hormones

Schedule 5 Controlled Drug POM

This can include POM or P medications depending on the licencing. They do not require any record-keeping on the balance available. CD prescription writing requirements as stated in the Misuse of Drugs Regulations 2001 do not apply. The prescriber does not have to be from the UK. A license is not required for import and export

Legal Requirements of Prescriptions

- State the issue date on the prescription
- Should be written legibly in indelible ink
- Signed by the issuing prescriber
- State the name and address of the prescriber
- State the name and address of the patient
- State the age of the patient if they are under 12 years
- Qualification/type of prescriber

Prescribers Signature

For computer-generated prescriptions a signature is acceptable. However, the prescriber's signature must still be handwritten, unless they use an advanced electronic signature, which is also legally valid. Especially with the 'Electronic Prescription Service' (EPS) in primary care.

Prescriptions are usually valid for a period of 6 months from the date that the prescription was issued.

Prescription Requirements for Schedule 2 and 3 Controlled Drugs

- Prescriptions that are written for controlled drugs have additional legal and professional requirements.

- A prescription for a schedule 2, 3, or 4 CD is valid for up to 28 days from the signed date.

- Schedule 5 prescriptions are valid for 6 months from the signed date.

- To avoid any misinterpretation and miscommunication the name of the requested drug must be written in full without any abbreviations.

- The maximum quantity of a schedule 2, 3 or 4 CD prescribed should not exceed a treatment period of 30 days. However, in exceptional circumstances, where there is a reasonable clinical need for the patient. In such cases, consider the benefits and risks of supplying more of the CD over a longer period, record your reasoning on the patient's record and then issue accordingly.

- The total quantity of a CD requested on a prescription must be written in words and figures.

- It is good practice to prescribe by brand for preparations which contain multi-constituents.

- The form/preparation of the drug must be specified on the prescription, for example, the prescription may state tablets, capsules, oral liquids, modified release/gastro-resistant tablets, solution for injection ampoules, suppositories, pessaries, eye/eye drops or transdermal patches.

- The strength of the medicine must also be stated to avoid ambiguity even if only one strength is available.

- Drugs co-prescribed with controlled drugs that are not CDs should not be prescribed on the same form as a Schedule 2 or 3 CD.

- The RX must also state the dose and frequency for the patient's instructions. With 'as required' directions, the minimum dose interval must be specified along with the maximum daily dose.

- The person collecting the schedule 2 or 3 CD from the pharmacy must sign the back of the prescription form and present a valid form of identification.

- If a CD prescription is issued by a dentist, then the following words should be stated on the RX 'for dental treatment only'.

Other Factors to Consider

For medications that should be taken over a specific period, such as antibiotics or reducing regimens, the prescription should specify the duration of the intended therapy.
- The total quantity to be supplied can be written explicitly or stated by indicating the number of days of treatment that should last.

Prescribers!

Good Practice Recommendations for Prescription Writing

- State the age and weight of the patient.

- State the patient's NHS/identification number

- State the contact details of the prescriber, e.g. the telephone number/email address

- State clear directions, ideally in English, although Latin abbreviations can also be used

- State units in full rather than abbreviations, for example state milligrams for mg or litres for L

- This avoids any ambiguity, especially when the 'L' and the number 1, may not be easily distinguishable

- Where a dose or strength is less than 1g, it should be written in milligrams e.g., amoxicillin 500mg, not 0.5g

- Where a dose or strength is less than 1mg, it should be written in micrograms e.g., write clonazepam 500 micrograms, not '0.5mg'

- Avoid any excessive use of decimal points on an RX, e.g., 10☐mg, not 10.0☐mg

Retaining Pharmacy Records

Pharmacy record retention is vital for legal compliance and audit purposes. Below is a summary of the minimum requirements for this, although local policy requirements may vary. This follows the guide of pharmacy record management by the 'Department of Health and Social Care' (DHSC).

- Clinical governance records should be kept for 5 years

- Patient survey data must be kept for 5 years

- Patient complaint data must be kept for 10 years

- Medicines reconciliation records should be kept for 2 years

- Completed CD registers must be kept for 2 years after the last entry

- CD requisitions must be kept 2 years

- CD destruction records should be kept for 7 years as good practice

- CD invoices must be kept for 6 years

- Medicinal recall data/documentation must be retained for 5 years

- A responsible pharmacist record book must be kept for 5 years

- Pharmacy minor incident/near-miss records must be kept for 10 years

- Community pharmacy clinical protocols should be kept for 25 years

- Wholesale dealing records should be kept for 5 years as part of good distribution practice

- Non-hazardous waste transfer consignments should be kept for 2 years

- Peer review records should be kept for at least a year for reference purposes.

- Unlicensed medicines dispensing records should be kept for 5 years

- Chemotherapy prescriptions should be kept for 2 years after the last treatment cycle has been issued (secondary/tertiary care setting)

- Under consumer liability legislation all quality control records must be kept for 5 years

- Community pharmacy patient medical records should be kept for 10 years after (even after the patient's death/left)

- The prescription only medication register should be kept for 2 years from the last entry

- Public health campaign participation records should be kept for 2 years

- MUR and NMS records must be kept for 2 years

- AUR records need to be kept for 1 year

- NHS CPCS records need to be kept for 2 years

- Community pharmacy influenza vaccination service records must be retained for at least 2 years

- Minor ailment service / Smoking cessation service / NHS health check / Substance misuse service forms must be kept for 2 years

Situational Judgement Test (SJT) Guidance

Confidentiality

As a pharmacy student, you are expected to represent the profession and uphold certain professional standards; one of which consists of confidentiality. Patients have the right to maintain their information between themselves and their healthcare professionals. Pharmacists and pharmacy students must treat all patients with respect for their private information. The General Pharmaceutical Council (GPhC) expects all graduating pharmacy students, to know 'how to maintain confidentiality'. Pharmacy students will not be expected to know all the intricacies of confidentiality, or the protocols associated with its breaches. However, they should still know the importance of confidentiality and how to respond to breaches of confidentiality, whether intentional or otherwise. As with other guides, this guide will cover what the GPhC states about confidentiality, the common scenarios you will come across and how to respond to them.

Printed on GPhC publications are the duties of pharmacists registered with the GPhC, one of which is to 'treat patients as individuals and respect their dignity', this includes an instruction to 'respect patients' right to confidentiality'.

From the GPhC publication *'Standards for Pharmacy Professionals'* **there are four main points regarding confidentiality that you should consider:**

- 'You must keep records containing personal information about patients, colleagues, or others securely, and in line with any data protection requirements

- 'You must treat information about patients as confidential. This includes after a patient has died'

- 'When publicly communicating, including speaking to, or writing in the media, you must maintain patient confidentiality. You should remember when using social media that communications intended for friends or family may become more widely available'

- 'You must cooperate with formal inquiries and complaints procedures and must offer all relevant information while following the guidance of confidentiality'

These points are not only relevant to registered pharmacists, but to all students involved with patients. The first point is particularly relevant to scenarios covering students or pharmacists making notes on patients and taking them home. As a further example, the third point is particularly relevant to discussions with the public or on social media. You should consider if you are the relevant person to be discussing a particular topic and remember that social media is a very common way for students to inadvertently publish identifiable information about a patient.

As a pharmacy professional, you should assume confidentiality applies unless you are told otherwise. There are a few scenarios, outlined in the GPhC's *Confidentiality* guideline, which is not necessary for you to read yet, but which may be of interest, where a breach of confidentiality is permissible. The most obvious case is when the patient has given consent. In other cases, the law obliges pharmacists to breach confidentiality if there is a potential risk to society. For example, a pharmacist is obliged to inform the DVLA if a patient has had seizures and has not reported them, as that is a risk to themselves and other drivers.

As a healthcare professional, your responsibility is to be vigilant and not to share patient information which identifies them with anyone not involved in their direct care. If you do need to share information with someone involved in the patient's care, only the required information should be given, and this should ideally be done in a private area, as 'many improper disclosures are unintentional'. Avoid discussion of confidential information in public areas. Even though you might not mention someone by name, there may be others nearby who recognise the patient by your description and learn something they should not have been privy to.

Main issues in confidentiality
- Publication on social media
- Loud discussions in public places
- Taking confidential information home
- Being asked for information

Dealing with Confidentiality:
With any breach of confidentiality, you have three important tasks:

Top confidentiality priorities:
1. Stop the breach as soon as possible
2. Do not draw attention to the event, i.e., deal with it discreetly, as drawing attention might further impact trust in the profession
3. Prevent any future breaches

The most appropriate responses will include all of the above. Context is important and every scenario will be different. For example, if you can discreetly and immediately stop a breach, waiting until later would be inappropriate. However, if you are unable to stop a breach immediately it is still very appropriate to speak to the relevant person later and explain what they did wrong.

It is very appropriate to:
- Ask the person who is breaching confidentiality to stop (to prevent breach)
- Find a private place in which to tell someone what they did wrong
- Explain why confidentiality is important
- Return any confidential information as soon as possible
- Inform the patient about the breach
- Apologise
- Report any mistake, with notes, to the appropriate authorities
- Resolve the problem locally without escalation
- Suggest that the person who has caused the problem talk to their supervisor about confidentiality
- Ask the patient whether they mind discussing their situation with someone else

It is typically appropriate, but not always ideal to:
- Distract people's attention to change the subject. Be careful with this, as changing the subject in some circumstances may be very appropriate, whereas in others it may not. The difference depends on the context and the extent to which you are drawing attention.
- Confront the person about the breach. This will solve the problem in a very direct and potentially aggressive manner that may be unnecessary. Talking more calmly may be just as effective.
- Return confidential information later. Ideally, you must ensure that the breach is minimal,

and that the data is returned as soon as possible.

In contrast to the above, it would be inappropriate to:

- Ignore the issue, for whatever reason
- Wait to see if the person does it again; this is inappropriate as the problem must not be allowed to escalate
- Expect someone else to solve the problem
- Dispose of confidential information yourself
- Blame someone else
- Avoid the patient
- Worry about the patient's opinion
- Tell someone confidential information either without permission or assuming permission; just because someone is a family member does not mean the patient wishes them to know their problem

Professional behaviour

As a pharmacy student, you will be required to maintain standards that many other university students are not held for. This is because, even as a student, you are recognised as a member of a profession that holds the public trust, which enables pharmacists to work as they do. As such, it is important you uphold the trust of healthcare professionals in what you do and strive to be an outstanding student. This involves being honest, attending all required teaching, treating people fairly and equitably, showing a desire to improve and maintaining a good reputation with your peers and community. Therefore, behaviours that go against these aims are inappropriate.

Note: We have covered some of these topics, such as cheating and drug misuse, in other guides. This guide will focus on general professional behaviour in the life of a pharmacy student/professional.

According to the GPhC, 'a pharmacist's behaviour must justify the trust that patients and the public have in them' and 'it is important to remember the need to behave professionally outside the university and work premises too'. While unprofessional behaviour 'could lead to fitness to practise proceedings, a pharmacy professional should not just behave professionally because of the threat of disciplinary proceedings, but to uphold the trust of the public in the profession that they are now a part of.

A few key relevant examples of unprofessional behaviour are summarised below.

Unprofessional behaviour summary
- Being uncommitted to work, lacking engagement and having poor attendance

- Failure to accept and follow advice and unwillingness to learn from feedback given by others

- Neglect of administrative tasks and poor time management

- Being rude or disruptive

- Any form of harassment or bullying

- Aggressive behaviour

Dealing with such situations can be quite complex; for example, approaching a colleague to tell them to change their behaviour can be daunting and picking your words carefully is important to get your point across without further problems.

As a pharmacy professional faced with these situations of others' unprofessionalism, your task is to maintain professional behaviour throughout the scenario and help others do the same. With any form of rudeness or offensive material, for example, your approach should be to stop the situation and prevent it from happening again.

More specifically, your goal should be to talk to the person and explain the situation, how they are being rude or why a joke or comment is offensive. The ideal situation would be for them to realise their mistake and apologise to the people whose feelings have been hurt. However, in doing this, you should make sure you are not being rude yourself or drawing more attention to the scene than necessary, which is likely to cause more problems rather than being part of the solution.

Note: Apologising does not mean taking the blame for something but is a way of saying 'I'm sorry you went through that'. The apology should come from them, but it is not inappropriate for you to offer an apology too.

Responding to someone being rude by being rude yourself is not a solution to the problem. Instead, it creates even more issues as the person is unlikely to respond well to your criticism and it could escalate into a public fight tarnishing the reputation of the health profession even further.

Appropriate responses aim to deal with any scenario calmly and reasonably. In some cases, this can mean waiting for an opportunity to privately speak to someone. Even if you are being considerate, cutting someone off in front undermines them and creates further problems for them and the image of the profession. You should not wait for them to do it again, which is inappropriate but instead wait for the next opportune moment.

In summary, it is appropriate to:
- Talk to someone in private about their offensive behaviour
- Apologise; probably appropriate, but not ideal
- Avoid further escalation
- Explain why a joke/comment is offensive
- Encourage people to speak to their supervisor
- Report unprofessional behaviour; (context-dependent)

In contrast, it is inappropriate to:
- Be rude or unprofessional, even when dealing with rude or unprofessional colleagues
- Cause a scene in front of patients
- Embarrass or undermine other colleagues in front of patients
- Ignore offensive comments or other forms of unprofessional behaviour
- Wait to see if people do something inappropriate again before acting
- Leave planning or doing work to the last minute
- Be inconsiderate of the workload that others face
- Expect people to accommodate you without notice

Important factors to consider are:
- That patients may be watching
- Patient safety
- The trust patients have in their pharmacists
- University/work policy
- That pharmacy students need to remain professional

Unimportant factors are:
- Reputation

- The other students/colleagues have done something like this before
- The person at fault is your friend or you might not know them very well
- There are others around who could talk to them
- No one will find out if you did not attend class

Teamwork

Throughout your professional career you will be expected to work closely with students, doctors, pharmacists, nurses and other healthcare professionals. As such, being a team player and working efficiently in a team setting are among the most important skills you must attain. One of the duties of a pharmacist, according to the GPhC, is to 'work with colleagues in the ways that best serve patients' interests. This can only be achieved with appropriate communication and compromise. You must understand important concepts such as the inclusion of all members of a team by allowing everyone to express an opinion, compromise on personal opinions, unless patient safety is involved, and the fair delegation and sharing of tasks.

Teamwork Summary

- 'You must work collaboratively with colleagues, respecting their skills and contributions.'
- 'You must treat colleagues fairly and with respect.'
- 'You must be aware of how your behaviour may influence others within and outside the team.'

These are important aspects of teamwork that apply in all settings, not just in hospitals.

Common scenarios in teamwork
- Someone feels left out
- Someone takes charge and pushes their opinion on others
- Someone is not doing their assigned work or is unprepared for meetings
- Someone has been unfairly burdened with too much work
- There are personal disagreements between team members
- There is conflict about team decisions, e.g. member 1 wants to do topic A, but member 2 wants to do topic B

While there will be multiple minor variations, regardless of the scenario, your approach should always be to reduce tension, present reasonable solutions, be fair, and support more marginalised members of the group. This will be covered in more detail on the next page.

Although group projects are common, there may be non-project situations or even a clinical setting.

In any teamwork scenario, your role, as a leader or member, is to do the following:

Key points
A) Make sure everyone has a voice/can express their opinion
B) Ensure that work is evenly distributed
C) Avoid conflict
D) Reduce any tensions
E) Support group decisions
F) Make sure the work is completed on time

Essentially, you want the team to work well together to achieve the desired goal. Any reasonable steps to support the above would typically be appropriate. The main exception is escalating to a senior member of staff, which is typically 'inappropriate, but not awful'. Referring the matter to be resolved by a senior member should be a last resort after the team has completely failed to settle its differences. In a way, escalating means that as a team you were not successful in working together and so did not address any of the points above. Instead, you are asking someone in authority to deal with those issues. There are some cases, as a last resort, where escalation is appropriate, but it should not be your first thought.

It is very appropriate to:
- Raise concerns about a problem politely
- Offer suggestions that will directly, or sometimes indirectly, solve the problem
- Make sure everyone shares their opinion
- Speak to people in private to find out what is concerning them
- Try to accommodate people where possible and appropriate
- Compromise to reach a common decision

Note: In the first point, you are told to raise concerns 'politely'. In a team context, confrontation is considered appropriate, but not ideal. This is because you are still raising an important point and possibly leading to an issue being resolved, but you could have done it in a more appropriate, less conflict-driven manner. Context is important, so consider whether your action is likely to embarrass someone in front of the whole group, which is not ideal, and would lead to more confrontation.

Example:
Consider a situation where a team member has come unprepared to the team meeting.

Here are some possible responses, with the most appropriate given first:

□ Ask to speak to the person in private to see if they are struggling with something.
□ Pull them to one side to explain that they are not doing enough to help the team.
□ Confront them in front of the group about not doing enough work.
□ Pointedly yell that some people don't care enough about the project.

These reactions to the situation of an ill-prepared team-mate go from constructive and understanding to disruptive and with less interest in finding a solution. It is not surprising if sometimes your classmates and team-mates will face problems that affect their work. Talking to them about their problems might lead to a solution more effectively than just explaining to them that they are not doing enough. The third option is not ideal, although still appropriate, as you are embarrassing them in public and have not asked why they have not done the work. The last option, which is inappropriate, offers no solution or constructive criticism and instead just lets you make your general frustrations known.

Inappropriate actions by a team member include:

- Ignoring concerns, whether they are yours or someone else's
- Creating conflict
- Allowing personal issues to affect the group
- Not cooperating with the group effort
- Not doing the work assigned to you
- Reassigning tasks without informing people
- Giving people more work than is fair
- Not allowing people to share their opinion
- Escalating unnecessarily
- Forcing someone or allowing yourself to be forced to do something you don't agree with, especially in a professional context
- Excluding people

The most important considerations are those that directly involve working successfully as a team and the assigned work/deadline. Patient safety is always a very important consideration and there should be a very good reason if it is not treated as such.

Examples of important considerations are:
- Patients might be at risk
- The project needs to be completed by a certain date
- One team member has concerns/has not had a chance to share their opinion

Dealing with patients
Professional behaviour is at the core of the GPhC's guidance on behaviour around patients. Pharmacists are meant to be respectful and considerate, build up trust with patients and do their best to help patients if they 'recognise and work within the limits of their competence'.

Your behaviour towards patients is highlighted in multiple segments in *'Standards for Pharmacy Professionals'*:

Dealing with patients
- You must be polite and considerate
- You must treat patients as individuals and respect their dignity and privacy
- You must treat patients fairly and with respect whatever their life choices and beliefs
- You must work in partnership with patients, sharing with them the information they will need to make decisions about their care

This approach is important in developing rapport with patients, maintaining their trust in you and the profession, and a general requirement of professional behaviour. Meanwhile, you also have a job to do (that is, to provide a healthcare service), and the GPhC also refers to being honest in your skills and working within your limits, such as:

- You must be honest and trustworthy in all your communication with patients and colleagues. Make clear the limits of your knowledge and make reasonable checks to ensure any information you give is accurate.

This is an important tenet of pharmacy practice and is included as one of the key duties of pharmacists, along with the following:

- Make the care of your patient your first concern

- Provide a good standard of practice and care

- Although you are not yet qualified, this principle applies to pharmacy students as well. If you do not know how to do them you are expected to learn, because you will hopefully qualify at some point in the future.

- If you are not sure you can carry out a task competently, you should ask for help from a more experienced qualified colleague.

- You should only attempt tasks; you have been trained to do

- If you think you are not being properly supervised on a placement, you should stop the work you are doing and raise your concerns.

- To take prompt action if you have any concerns about possible risks to patients.

- You must be honest in financial and commercial dealings with patients.

- You must not allow any interests you have to affect the way you prescribe for, treat, refer or commission services for patients.

- If you are faced with a conflict of interest, you must be open about the conflict, declaring your interest formally, and you should be prepared to exclude yourself from decision-making.

- You must not ask for or accept, from patients, colleagues or others, any inducement, gift or hospitality that may affect or be seen to affect the way you prescribe for, treat or refer patients or commission services for patients. You must not offer these inducements.

It is clarified you may accept unsolicited gifts from patients or their relatives if this does not clash with the principles outlined above. However, it is important, to 'consider the potential damage this could cause to your patient's trust in you and the public's trust in the profession' and 'you should refuse gifts or bequests where they could be perceived as an abuse of trust'. Throughout the guide, the GPhC advises honesty about such situations, using professional judgement to decide if conflicts exist and seeking advice if in doubt. Finally, 'If you are in doubt about whether there is a conflict of interest, act as though there is.'

We have mentioned that GPhC allows gifts but asks you to consider the impact they may have. Many healthcare trusts have their policy about staff accepting gifts, such as setting a value limit on gifts that staff can accept. You do not have to know every rule about accepting gifts, but your response to gifts in patient-related scenarios may depend on what the policy is. Typically, either you will be told what the policy is, or the policy will not affect your response. In all cases, whether you can accept a gift or not, remember to be respectful and honest. It is always very appropriate to explain to the patient why you might not be able to accept a gift but thank them regardless.

Common scenarios in dealing with patients

- Angry patient, e.g., a patient accuses someone or confronts a member of staff about waiting times
- Distressed patient, e.g., a patient in discomfort during a procedure
- Confused patient, e.g., an elderly patient who looks lost in the ward
- General consultation, e.g., discussing medication options, arranging appointments, or creating a care plan
- Gifts and money from patients

Depending on each instance, you might have to respond to the situation as a pharmacy student, trainee or pharmacist. This is important to keep in mind, as your capabilities and what you can do are quite different. As a pharmacy student/trainee, you do not have a licence to practice, so it is not appropriate by any means to act as a pharmacist and offer medical advice or perform procedures without supervision or at least be sent by a relevant professional with appropriate consent.

It is generally very appropriate to:

- Listen to concerns from all sides
- Avoid placing blame or favouring any side without clear evidence
- Prioritise appropriately based on the relative risk to patients and the urgency
- Be honest and up front with patients
- Be aware of your limitations and not exceed them

- Offer patients any information they need or request, that you can provide, not forgetting confidentiality
- Offer to find out more information or find someone responsible to better resolve the situation
- Act according to the policy
- Respect informed consent
- To be respectful

In contrast, it is not appropriate to:
- Act unprofessionally
- Be rude to patients
- Waste other people's time
- Go beyond your capabilities
- Ignore the situation
- Continue a procedure when a patient is distressed or asks you to stop
- Make promises you cannot or might not be able to keep

Dealing with mistakes
We all make mistakes at various points in our lives or our daily activities. Yet in the pharmacy profession mistakes can have very serious consequences for patient health and well-being. While mistakes happen, it is an important part of medical practice to check for mistakes, understand why they happened and put procedures in place to avoid them in the future. In an exam setting, you must show an understanding of the appropriate response to a mistake.

Dealing with mistakes is one of the more difficult things in the healthcare profession; as the GPhC acknowledges, mistakes can be scary to deal with, both for the questions it raises about your competence as a pharmacist and for the fear of repercussions. However, pharmacists cannot learn from their mistakes if they are not recognised and acted on. Furthermore, patients have a right to know what happened to them and this is at the core of practice. One of the core duties of a pharmacist, as the GPhC succinctly puts it, is to:

Be honest, and open and act with integrity.

This is the core tenet when considering your mistakes; dealing with mistakes any other way would go against this principle and be unethical.

The GPhC expands on this:

'You must be open and honest with patients if things go wrong. If a patient under your care has suffered harm or distress, you should:

- A. Put matters right, if possible
- B. Offer an apology
- C. Explain fully and promptly what has happened and the likely short-term and long-term effects.'

A few further steps are covered in the guidance entitled

'Openness and Honesty When Things go Wrong: The Professional Duty of Candour'.

As a pharmacist, you should quickly report mistakes or near-misses, as required by policy, to avoid further harm and to allow appropriate procedures to be put in place.

Common scenarios you may face in an exam/interview

1. You have made a mistake or almost made a mistake.
2. A senior has made a mistake or almost made a mistake, and you noticed it.

Consider the following scenario

Jane is a trainee pharmacist on a ward round with her consultant, Dr Smith. During the ward round, Dr Smith prescribes an antibiotic for Ms Hugo. While checking her notes after the ward round, Jane realises Ms Hugo is allergic to that antibiotic. Dr Smith has left for a conference and is currently unavailable.

In this scenario, Jane faces two problems: the prescription error and the fact Dr Smith is no longer available. This is a difficult scenario to deal with, as you must balance teamwork and the matter of dealing with a mistake that has been made.

As we have mentioned in other guides, the distinction between scenario types can be blurred by the simple fact that healthcare, and life in general, is multi-faceted and influenced by multiple factors.

Now consider this scenario

Robindo is a junior pharmacist on his surgical rotation, working on an oncology ward looking after Mr Surinder. Robindo is well-regarded by his colleagues and his supervisor seems very pleased with the consistency and punctuality of his work, having praised him for being thorough. During the ward round, the consultant asked Mr Surinder to be prepared for surgery and this task fell upon the oncology team and Robindo. Arriving on the ward the next morning, Robindo realises that he forgot to prepare Mr Surinder's medications before surgery.

This scenario deals with a mistake, namely not preparing Mr Surinder for surgery, but involves a lot of teamwork aspects. Robindo made a mistake that does not impact just him but his team also.

Generally, the aim should be to:
- Apologise to the patient
- Report the mistake as per university/hospital policy, often including near misses
- Fix the mistake as soon as you can within reasonable limits

The last point is very important, as the 'limits' will change depending on the scenario. If you are a pharmacist, you might be able to change a prescription to another drug that has the same effect, but as a pharmacy student, you do not have the knowledge, skill or, most importantly, the authority to do this. The other aspect you need to consider when fixing a mistake is that doing so does not mean rushing to a solution, as that can lead to more mistakes and is generally an inappropriate response.

The two options you will be given are that:
- A mistake has happened
- A mistake might have happened

The difference is the level of certainty in the witnesses. For example, if you know someone is allergic to a drug and they have received it in a prescription, a mistake has occurred. There is no doubt about what has happened. Elsewhere, a mistake may be more technical and there may be uncertainty about whether an event is a mistake. An observer may be mistaken and just because something is different does not mean it is wrong.

For example, Paul is a junior pharmacist watching his senior pharmacist carrying out a medicine reconciliation. The patient is awake and watching the pharmacists with interest. During the process, Paul notices the senior pharmacist has added one of the patients' medications to the drug chart that should have been stopped this morning.

In this instance, there are two factors at play: the potential mistake and the fact that the patient is watching; the patient watching complicates the scenario as you do not want to damage patient trust in the healthcare team, be it the senior pharmacist making a mistake or you for erroneously calling the senior colleague out. Paul is a junior and should rightly raise his concerns about a possible mistake, but he must do it in a way that does not lead to unnecessary embarrassment and cause further problems.

Consider the difference between asking the senior pharmacist why he added the medication back on the drug chart compared with telling the patient, in front of the senior pharmacist, that a mistake has been made and it will be immediately fixed.

In the first instance, Paul finds out if there was an actual mistake without unsettling the patient; he is a junior and is seemingly asking his senior about a procedure. If there is a mistake, the senior pharmacist will be made aware and if there is not and the senior pharmacist made a conscious decision to act in that way then Paul will receive an explanation.
Finally, consider the level of seriousness of the mistake. There is a big difference between a student making a mistake and a registered professional making a medical error. In both cases, you should raise your concerns but there is less urgency in the first scenario.

Appropriate and Inappropriate Actions

It is appropriate to:
- Apologise to the patient and explain what happened
- Ask a senior for advice if unsure what to do
- Appropriately fix the mistake
- Report the incident
- Raise concerns about mistakes
- Avoid causing panic and remain calm
- Find out what caused the mistake

In contrast, it is inappropriate to:
- Ignore mistakes or accept that they happen
- Not report them, even if they did not actually cause harm or were spotted
- Ignore policy
- Do something you are not licensed for or competent at

Most important factors:
- Patient safety
- The patient's right to know what happened
- Hospital policy

Factors that are not important are:
- No one noticed the error
- The person responsible is not available
- Someone else is superior in rank
- The person responsible has power over you or is marking your work
- Someone else may notice the mistake and fix it
- It was a minor mistake
- It was a near-miss

Drug misuse

Working in the healthcare profession can be very stressful and, for whatever reason, people may end up abusing alcohol or illegal substances. While illegal substance or alcohol misuse is not good for anyone, it can have even more severe consequences when the person is a pharmacist or a healthcare professional. This is because a pharmacist is responsible for lives other than their own and drug abuse can affect their ability to safely deal with patients

Dealing with drug abuse falls under professional behaviour, but this aspect of professionalism can be confusing to people, so we wrote this guide to clarify how to approach this kind of scenario.

GPhC's five points of concern

1. Driving under the influence of alcohol or drugs
2. Abusing prescription medication
3. Alcohol consumption that affects clinical work/performance
4. Dealing, possessing, supplying or misusing drugs
5. A pattern of excessive misuse of alcohol

You should report people for alcohol abuse.
The GPhC state:

'If you have concerns that a colleague may not be fit to practise and maybe put patients at risk, you must ask for advice from a colleague, your defence body or us. If you are still concerned you must report this, in line with our guidance and your workplace policy, and make a record of the steps you have taken.'

Whereas in other scenarios, such as teamwork, we have said it is better to deal with the situation locally before escalating, as escalating might even be inappropriate, but that is not the case here. If you feel that a colleague is putting patients at risk by their abusive behaviour you are expected to escalate the matter and should report your concerns to a senior or as outlined by policy.

Drug and alcohol abuse is a very serious issue and deciding how to approach and deal with it in real life can be very challenging legally, ethically and procedurally.

Common scenarios of drug/alcohol abuse

- A colleague smells of alcohol at work or is witnessed in the act of consuming alcohol or drugs in the workplace.
- Hints or obvious signs a person's work and general life are impaired, e.g., dishevelled appearance, lack of focus, falling behind on work, etc.
- The person tries to hide the problem.

The appropriate approach to these scenarios involves protecting patients, providing help and seeing if the person is willing to accept help, and, if patient safety is a concern, which it typically is, raising concerns with seniors. When unsure, it is always appropriate to ask discreetly for advice.

A major point to note about raising concerns, not just in this type of scenario but in others as well (e.g., cheating), is escalation, this does not mean spreading information to everyone. Only the relevant people should be told. Avoid spreading rumours, this is inappropriate and not recommended.
Other inappropriate responses include ignoring the issue, creating havoc while responding to it, or being judgemental or discriminatory.

Top priorities surrounding drug abuse
- Patient safety
- The person might need help
- Being discreet
- Hospital policy
- The public's trust in the medical profession

In general, keep in mind how this behaviour can affect patients and let that guide your responses to these scenarios. At this point, understanding that misuse is a fitness-to-practise concern and reporting is appropriate to protect patients and colleagues.

Cheating
Cheating is another aspect of professional behaviour that is unacceptable. Like drug misuse, cheating is handled in specific ways as it relates to a person's fitness to practise.

The GPhC is very clear that cheating and dishonesty will put a student's fitness to practise under scrutiny.

In publications, the GPhC gives some examples of what constitutes cheating/plagiarism, although this is not an exhaustive list:
- Cheating in examinations
- Signing peers into taught sessions from which they are absent from
- Passing off the work of others as one's own
- Sharing with fellow students, or others, details of questions or tasks from exams
- Forging a supervisor's name or falsifying feedback on assessments

Cheating is not only relevant to your role as a pharmacy student, but to all your professional undertakings. This includes falsifying research, making fraudulent claims on your CV or misrepresenting your qualifications. All these raise questions about a student's honesty, trustworthiness and character and, as such, are reasons for concern.

Coping with pressure

Nobody is immune to pressure or difficulty and, as a pharmacy student or professional, you may find yourself in situations where you are under a lot of pressure. This may be from exams, struggling to keep up with responsibilities, going through a difficult period emotionally, e.g., a break-up or a close family member passing away, or life in general. As a healthcare professional, your ability to practise is influenced by your health and mental state.

If you are struggling to cope or otherwise become physically or mentally unwell, it can have a serious impact on patient health and/or wellbeing. As such, the GPhC has highlighted in multiple publications the importance of looking after yourself and dealing with stress. In this guide, we will cover what the GPhC mention about looking after yourself, and what you are expected to do in pressured situations.

Your ability to practise is influenced by physical or mental health difficulties and it is your responsibility to make sure you take appropriate action to seek help and look after yourself. In standards produced by the GPhC, they establish health as one of the core principles of professional practice, stating *'pharmacy professionals must not allow their health or condition to put patients at risk'*.

If a professional knows or suspects that they have a serious condition that could pass on to patients, or if judgement or performance could be affected by a condition or its treatment, a suitably qualified colleague must be informed.

Summary points
- Look after your health and that of your colleagues
- Seek help if in trouble
- Support others in trouble
- It is not acceptable to excuse people's behaviour because of the pressure they are facing

Common scenarios of pressure
- Feeling pressure or being nervous about a particular activity
- Life events that influence one's emotional state
- Juggling different obligations

When dealing with pressure yourself, note the appropriateness of the following responses:

It is most appropriate to:
1. Recognise the problem
2. Talk to someone about the problem
3. Seek help from a responsible/suitable person
4. Raise the issue with the appropriate members of staff so alternative arrangements can be made
5. Work with others to reach a compromise

On the other hand, it is inappropriate to:
- Ignore the situation (very inappropriate)
- Ignore your responsibilities
- Not inform anyone of the problems you face
- Place a greater work burden on others

- Be rude to people around you
- Ignore university policy

A highly context-dependent situation involves dealing with other responsibilities or commitments you have. However, it is important and appropriate to discuss the issue with the people you have made that commitment to and agree to a compromise or at least inform them about your inability to continue.

The most important considerations are your health and being able to cope with pressure. Other conflicting factors can have an impact, but the relevant importance is highly context dependent. You may have other responsibilities you are committed to, but these clearly do not take precedence over your education or your well-being. Your reputation or any concerns about how you will be perceived by your supervisors are not important at all, and your seeking help will not affect their judgement of you.

When giving advice and helping someone else cope with pressure, note the appropriateness of the following:

It is typically appropriate to:
1. Recognise and acknowledge the problems they face
2. Provide reassurance
3. Offer help to the extent you are permitted or able to

While it is very appropriate to suggest someone speak to a counsellor about problems they are facing, it is very inappropriate as a pharmacy trainee to; for example, suggest medication such as anti-depressants, as they are not a suitable person and lack the qualifications to offer that support. It is also not advisable for prescribers to give prescriptions to friends and family.

It is inappropriate to:
- Leave people alone in a crisis: in these situations, it is far more appropriate to ask someone else to bring senior help
- Ignore the problem
- Expect someone else to act for you
- Remind them of their commitments: this is typically inappropriate, but not awful. However, depending on the context, it can be very inappropriate as it does not help the situation at all and can exaggerate the person's stress.

Section 1
Situational Judgmental Test Questions

1. Stanley and Rinky are pharmacy students in the same tutorial group. As part of the aseptic module, both students are required to complete a short assignment based on individually assigned reading for the next meeting of the tutorial group. Thirty minutes before the tutorial group meeting commences, Stanley asks Rinky if he can quickly look at Rinky's essay.

How **important** are the following considerations for Rinky to consider when deciding how to respond to the situation?

1A) The tutor asked each student to write their own essay.
Answer:
- A. Very important
- B. Important
- C. Of minor importance
- D. Not important at all

1B) That Stanley may react and behave negatively if Rinky declines his request to see the essay.
Answer:
- A. Very important
- B. Important
- C. Of minor importance
- D. Not important at all

1C) Stanley has asked to copy Rinky's coursework last year on a previous module.
Answer:
- A. Very important
- B. Important
- C. Of minor importance
- D. Not important at all

2. Sangeeta is a fourth-year pharmacy student interviewing a patient on her ward placement, Mr White, who is an inpatient in a hospital with serious but not life-threatening ailments. Sangeeta knows that the medical doctors are struggling to identify the causative aetiology of Mr White's symptoms. Mr White confides in Sangeeta that he purchased weight loss pills online and has been taking them but has been embarrassed to inform the doctors/nurses of this. Sangeeta realises that there is a strong possibility that the weight loss supplements are causing some, if not all, of Mr White's health problems.

How **important** are the following considerations for Sangeeta to consider when deciding how to respond to the situation?

2A) That the doctors do not know, Mr White has been taking the weight loss capsules.
Answer:
   A. Very important
   B. Important
   C. Of minor importance
   D. Not important at all

2B) That Sangeeta is not aware of the active ingredient in the capsules.
Answer:
   A. Very important
   B. Important
   C. Of minor importance
   D. Not important at all

2C) That the weight loss capsules may explain at least some of the patient's health problems.
Answer:
   A. Very important
   B. Important
   C. Of minor importance
   D. Not important at all

2D) That Mr White is embarrassed to tell the doctors about taking the weight loss capsules.
Answer:
   A. Very important
   B. Important
   C. Of minor importance
   D. Not important at all

3. Jonathan is a trainee pharmacist in the emergency department. When he steps into a bay to see the next patient, Jonathan realises that the patient is someone he used to know socially.

How **important** are the following considerations for **Jonathan** to consider when deciding how to respond to the situation?

3A) That Jonathan has not seen the patient socially in the last few years.
Answer:
   A. Very important
   B. Important
   C. Of minor importance
   D. Not important at all

3B) The patient does not seem to recognise Jonathan, even after he introduces himself.
Answer:
   A. Very important
   B. Important
   C. Of minor importance
   D. Not important at all

3C) The patient is bleeding and in severe amount of distress.
Answer:
   A. Very important
   B. Important
   C. Of minor importance
   D. Not important at all

3D) The patient is fully alert and capable of answering questions.
Answer:
   A. Very important
   B. Important
   C. Of minor importance
   D. Not important at all

4.   A third-year pharmacy student, Reeta, is in the process of undertaking interviews with patients in a hospital ward as part of her modular assignment. A patient in another part of the ward, Edith, waves at Reeta to come over to her bed and asks if she can be discharged tonight and go home. Edith states that she had an awful night's sleep in the ward last night prior to her surgery and that she would sleep better at home. Edith also states that the doctor had advised an overnight stay for observation, but Edith is feeling much better already. Edith is not one of the patients that Reeta has been assigned to interview.

How **important** are the following considerations for **Reeta** to consider when deciding how to respond to the situation?

4A) Edith is not one of the patients that Reeta has been assigned to interview.
Answer:
   A. Very important
   B. Important
   C. Of minor importance
   D. Not important at all

4B) The doctor said Edith should stay in the hospital overnight for observation.
Answer:
   A. Very important
   B. Important
   C. Of minor importance
   D. Not important at all

4C) Whether Edith can be aided in getting a better night's sleep in the hospital tonight.
Answer:
   A. Very important
   B. Important
   C. Of minor importance
   D. Not important at all

5. A newly qualified pharmacist, Lynne, has just started working in the paediatric ward. The ward nurses are very polite and professional with her during her first week. But then an article about Lynne is published in the hospital newsletter, in which she discusses her experiences as a lesbian pharmacist in the NHS. Lynne arrives on the ward the next day to find a group of nurses looking at the article and laughing. When Lynne asks them, what is so funny, the nurses say nothing. However, the nurses treat Lynne strangely for the rest of the

day, avoiding her when possible and giving the
briefest of responses.

How **important** are the following considerations for
Lynne to consider when deciding how to respond to
the situation?

5A) That Lynne may need to improve her working
relationships with the nurses on the ward.
Answer:
    A. Very important
    B. Important
    C. Of minor importance
    D. Not important at all

5B) That it would be best to avoid interacting with these
nurses for the rest of the day.
Answer:
    A. Very important
    B. Important
    C. Of minor importance
    D. Not important at all

5C) Whether the senior nurse on the ward is willing to
address the homophobia among the nurses.
Answer:
    A. Very important
    B. Important
    C. Of minor importance
    D. Not important at all

6. A fourth-year pharmacy student, Ronny, has
been affected by adverse weather conditions
and caught in a storm on the way to her
hospital placement. When Ronny arrives at the
hospital, her hair is messy and dishevelled and
her clothes are soaked. Ronny is due to attend
ward rounds at the start of her shift, which is
about to start, but she is concerned that her
current physical state would violate the

hospital's strict dress code by presenting herself to patients in such a state.
How **important** are the following considerations for **Ronny** to consider when deciding how to respond to the situation?

6A) The consultant leading the ward rounds will be displeased if Ronny arrives late.
Answer:
    A. Very important
    B. Important
    C. Of minor importance
    D. Not important at all

6B) Hospital scrubs are available in the locker room for staff to wear.
Answer:
    A. Very important
    B. Important
    C. Of minor importance
    D. Not important at all

6C) It will take a few minutes for Ronny to tidy her hair.
Answer:
    A. Very important
    B. Important
    C. Of minor importance
    D. Not important at all

6D) Ronny keeps a change of smart clothes in her locker at the hospital.
Answer:
    A. Very important
    B. Important
    C. Of minor importance
    D. Not important at all

7. A patient's relative asks Seema, a trainee pharmacist if she can accompany her elderly father in hospital transport to a specialist

hospital. Seema knows that the hospital policy only allows the transport of patients but can see that the patient is very distressed about being separated from his daughter.

How **important** are each of the following considerations for **Seema** when deciding how to respond to the situation?

7A) Hospital policy only allows patients to travel in hospital transport.
Answer:
    A. Very important
    B. Important
    C. Of minor importance
    D. Not important at all

7B) The patient is very distressed about being separated from his daughter.
Answer:
    A. Very important
    B. Important
    C. Of minor importance
    D. Not important at all

8. John, a third-year pharmacy student is completing a placement at a specialist care unit. John's father has requested him to bring a handful of personal protective equipment, including face masks and gloves from the care unit as they are running out at home. John knows that healthcare staff, patients and patient family members can take free masks from a supply at the entrance of the hospital but taking more than one free mask per day is prohibited. Any staff and visitors are expected to wear face masks in the hospital to reduce the spread of infections. However, John also does not want to disappoint his father.

How **important** are each of the following considerations for **John** when deciding how to respond to the situation?

8A) John's father is unable to afford to purchase new face masks and gloves due to financial difficulties.
Answer:
A. Important
B. Not important

8B) John has noticed other healthcare professionals take more than one free mask per day before.
Answer:
A. Important
B. Not important

8C) A shortage of masks at the hospital entrance could lead to a rise in infection transmission.
Answer:
A. Important
B. Not important

9. Pooja is a Pharmacy student carrying out her general practice placement. During a consultation, the lead GP suggests that the patient needs to have their blood taken, which the patient agrees to. The GP asks Pooja to take the patient's blood, whilst the patient is still in the room. Pooja has never taken blood before and has not reached a point in her education where she would have practised taking blood on a dummy. However, Pooja is concerned about declining the request, since the GP has been annoyed at Pooja before for not being competent in clinical skills.

How **appropriate** are each of the following considerations for **Pooja** when deciding how to respond to the situation?

9A) Explain that she has not practised taking blood before and does not feel comfortable doing so.
Answer:
- A. Appropriate
- B. Inappropriate

9B) Agree to take the patient's blood, asking the GP to guide her through the process step by step.
Answer:
- A. Appropriate
- B. Inappropriate

9C) Suggest that she will take blood from the next patient after observing the GP take blood from this patient.
Answer:
- A. Appropriate
- B. Inappropriate

10. A first-year pharmacy student, Jack, is completing a questionnaire with a patient in a hospital ward. The patient that Jack is about to interview has just been diagnosed with a serious terminal illness. The patient makes several comments about her personal religious beliefs and then asks Jack to join in prayer. The patient states that she wants to pray the illness away. Jack is not religious and is an atheist, thus is uncomfortable at being asked to join in prayer.

How **appropriate** are each of the following responses by **Jack** in this situation? Assume that each of the following responses would be said politely.

10A) "Would you like to discuss your concerns about your illness with one of the doctors/nurses or pharmacists?"
Answer:
- A. A very appropriate thing to do
- B. Appropriate but not ideal
- C. Inappropriate but not awful
- D. A very inappropriate thing to do

10B) "Sorry, it's not right for me to pray with you since you need to be made aware that I don't share your religious beliefs."
Answer:
- A. A very appropriate thing to do
- B. Appropriate but not ideal
- C. Inappropriate but not awful
- D. A very inappropriate thing to do

10C) "Do you have any questions about your diagnosis that I could share with the doctors?"
Answer:
- A. A very appropriate thing to do
- B. Appropriate but not ideal
- C. Inappropriate but not awful
- D. A very inappropriate thing to do

10D) "Let's focus on finishing the questions in this questionnaire and do your prayer later."
Answer:
- A. A very appropriate thing to do
- B. Appropriate but not ideal
- C. Inappropriate but not awful
- D. A very inappropriate thing to do

11. Dr Ralph is a consultant, partaking in a one-to-one meeting with Joshua, a newly qualified band-6 pharmacist on the ward. Near the end of the meeting, Joshua closes his notebook. Dr Ralph is shocked to see that Joshua has written the username and password for the

patient records database on the cover of his personal notebook.

How **appropriate** are each of the following responses by **Dr Ralph** in this situation? Assume that each of the following responses would be said politely.

11A) "We need to have a quick chat about the confidentiality of patient records."
Answer:
- A. A very appropriate thing to do
- B. Appropriate but not ideal
- C. Inappropriate but not awful
- D. A very inappropriate thing to do

11B) "Could you please ensure your notebook is locked away before you start working on the ward?"
Answer:
- A. A very appropriate thing to do
- B. Appropriate but not ideal
- C. Inappropriate but not awful
- D. A very inappropriate thing to do

11C) "Am I right that you have your login details for the patient records database on the front of your notebook?"
Answer:
- A. A very appropriate thing to do
- B. Appropriate but not ideal
- C. Inappropriate but not awful
- D. A very inappropriate thing to do

11D) "Please remove the top of your notebook and ensure it is shredded!"
Answer:
- A. A very appropriate thing to do
- B. Appropriate but not ideal
- C. Inappropriate but not awful
- D. A very inappropriate thing to do

12. Amir and Sanjay are third-year pharmacy students who are about to start working at the university pharmacy. They are required to attend fire safety training before commencing their placement. There is a large intake of students at the fire safety training, and Amir states that he does not see the point in attending as he thinks it's obvious what to do in a fire. Amir asks Sanjay to sign his name on the sign-in sheet of the training to get signed off.

How **appropriate** are each of the following responses by **Sanjay** in this situation? Assume that each of the following responses would be said politely.

12A) "Why don't you attend the first ten minutes of the training and see if there's any value in it?"
Answer:
    A. A very appropriate thing to do
    B. Appropriate but not ideal
    C. Inappropriate but not awful
    D. A very inappropriate thing to do

12B) "You should attend the training. There's probably a lot in it that you don't already know."
Answer:
    A. A very appropriate thing to do
    B. Appropriate but not ideal
    C. Inappropriate but not awful
    D. A very inappropriate thing to do

12C) "I'm not comfortable signing your name, or with you working in the campus pharmacy without fire safety training."
Answer:
    A. A very appropriate thing to do
    B. Appropriate but not ideal
    C. Inappropriate but not awful
    D. A very inappropriate thing to do

12D) "If you are going to miss the training, you should notify our tutor so they can let the pharmacy know."
Answer:
- A. A very appropriate thing to do
- B. Appropriate but not ideal
- C. Inappropriate but not awful
- D. A very inappropriate thing to do

13. A pharmacy student, Clare, is completing her placement in a hospital ward. When she is working in the ward, Claire must wear scrubs and a hospital name badge. An in-patient on the ward waves Claire over to his bed. Claire knows from a team meeting that the patient is scheduled for important surgery the next day. The patient says to Claire, 'Doctor, do I need the operation?' Claire hesitates before responding to the patient.

How **appropriate** are each of the following responses by **Claire** in this situation?

13A) Apologise for the confusion and explain that she is only a pharmacy student.
Answer:
- A. A very appropriate thing to do
- B. Appropriate but not ideal
- C. Inappropriate but not awful
- D. A very inappropriate thing to do

13B) Encourage the patient to raise the concerns with one of the doctors on the next ward rounds.
Answer:
- A. A very appropriate thing to do
- B. Appropriate but not ideal
- C. Inappropriate but not awful
- D. A very inappropriate thing to do

14. Mrs Pegg has been on the waiting list for a renal transplant. Mrs Pegg has asked her consultant, Linda, if there is anything she can do to move up the list. Mrs Pegg suggests paying, but Linda explains that this is illegal. On Linda's birthday, she finds a greeting card placed under her office door. The card has been given by Mrs Pegg and contains £2500 in cash. When Linda visits Mrs Pegg on the ward later that day, Mrs Pegg asks Linda if she received the birthday gift and whether there is anything she can do for her.

How **appropriate** are each of the following responses by **Linda** in this situation?

14A) Hand the cash back to the patient, explaining it is unethical for her to accept money from patients.
Answer:

        A. A very appropriate thing to do
        B. Appropriate but not ideal
        C. Inappropriate but not awful
        D. A very inappropriate thing to do

14B) Inform Mrs Pegg that if she continues to offer inducements, she will have to report her to the hospital authorities.
Answer:

        A. A very appropriate thing to do
        B. Appropriate but not ideal
        C. Inappropriate but not awful
        D. A very inappropriate thing to do

14C) Ask another colleague on the ward to take over this patient's care.
Answer:

        A. A very appropriate thing to do
        B. Appropriate but not ideal
        C. Inappropriate but not awful
        D. A very inappropriate thing to do

15. Arjun is a nursing student starting his first shift in the emergency department. The department is extremely busy, and Arjun has not yet had a chance to meet the doctor supervising his placement. A senior nurse informs Arjun that a patient needs blood drawn urgently. Arjun has never taken blood from a patient before and is quite nervous about being asked to do so for the first time without supervision.

How **appropriate** are each of the following responses by **Arjun** in this situation?

15A) Ask if he could speak to the doctor supervising his placement before drawing blood from a patient.
Answer:
- A. A very appropriate thing to do
- B. Appropriate but not ideal
- C. Inappropriate but not awful
- D. A very inappropriate thing to do

15B) Explain that he has never taken blood and feels uncomfortable doing so without supervision.
Answer:
- A. A very appropriate thing to do
- B. Appropriate but not ideal
- C. Inappropriate but not awful
- D. A very inappropriate thing to do

15C) Refuse to draw blood from the patient.
Answer:
- A. A very appropriate thing to do
- B. Appropriate but not ideal
- C. Inappropriate but not awful
- D. A very inappropriate thing to do

16. A trainee pharmacist, Nelly, was held up by excessive traffic this morning while commuting and is now running late for her placement at a GP surgery. Nelly arrives at the surgery to find a patient who uses a wheelchair, Gabbana, waiting outside. Some refurbishment works are underway on the building's front exterior, and as a result, the wheelchair ramp has been blocked by scaffolding. The main entrance can only be reached by three steps. Gabbana explains to Nelly that he could manage to climb the three steps with some assistance, but he is worried about leaving his wheelchair outside the surgery during his appointment.

How **appropriate** are each of the following responses by **Nelly** in this situation?

16A) Explain to Gabbana that she is running late, but she will let someone know that Gabbana is waiting outside.
Answer:

      A. A very appropriate thing to do
      B. Appropriate but not ideal
      C. Inappropriate but not awful
      D. A very inappropriate thing to do

16B) Apologise to the patient for the inconvenience.
Answer:

      A. A very appropriate thing to do
      B. Appropriate but not ideal
      C. Inappropriate but not awful
      D. A very inappropriate thing to do

16C) Ask the patient if he minds waiting while she pops inside to find someone to help.
Answer:

      A. A very appropriate thing to do
      B. Appropriate but not ideal
      C. Inappropriate but not awful
      D. A very inappropriate thing to do

17. A group of pharmacy undergraduate students are meeting to prepare their written report for a group project due next week. They will receive a shared grade for the project which will count towards each student's final grade. Each student has written a portion of the report. The group spends several minutes reading Ricky's portion of the report, and Nikita notices that Ricky's portion is riddled with errors, including many punctuation errors and run-on sentences, and several incorrect claims about the published research on their topic. Ricky asks for feedback, and the other group members say that it's good.

How **appropriate** are each of the following responses by **Nikita** in this situation?

17A) Suggest that some of the group members proofread the group's work before submitting the final report.
Answer:

      A. A very appropriate thing to do
      B. Appropriate but not ideal
      C. Inappropriate but not awful
      D. A very inappropriate thing to do

17B) Ask if the other group members have any more specific comments for Ricky on his portion of the report.
Answer:

      A. A very appropriate thing to do
      B. Appropriate but not ideal
      C. Inappropriate but not awful
      D. A very inappropriate thing to do

17C) Point out that their grades will suffer if they submit work that is full of errors.
Answer:
    A. A very appropriate thing to do
    B. Appropriate but not ideal
    C. Inappropriate but not awful
    D. A very inappropriate thing to do

18. Before the start of a busy day at an outpatient's anticoagulation clinic, the lead pharmacist approaches the staff kitchen where a junior pharmacist colleague is making a cup of tea. The junior pharmacist is talking to himself and laughing wildly at random intervals. Another member of staff told the lead pharmacist that the junior pharmacist was behaving strangely the day before, but the junior pharmacist's behaviour now seems far worse than the lead pharmacist was told. The lead pharmacist is concerned, as the junior pharmacist is about to start seeing patients in the next 10 minutes.

How **appropriate** are each of the following responses by **the lead pharmacist** in this situation?

18A) Ask the junior pharmacist how he is getting on with his work.
Answer:
    A. A very appropriate thing to do
    B. Appropriate but not ideal
    C. Inappropriate but not awful
    D. A very inappropriate thing to do

18B) Wait to see if the junior pharmacist continues to act strangely over the next hour.
Answer:
    A. A very appropriate thing to do
    B. Appropriate but not ideal
    C. Inappropriate but not awful
    D. A very inappropriate thing to do

18C) Make a note of the junior pharmacist's behaviour and the date and time it was observed.
Answer:

    A. A very appropriate thing to do
    B. Appropriate but not ideal
    C. Inappropriate but not awful
    D. A very inappropriate thing to do

19. A fourth-year pharmacy student, Lauren, is given the assignment to work with a general practitioner, Dr Thomas, for two weeks. The attachment is intended to give Lauren insights into Dr Thomas's work and to further Lauren's professional development. At the start of the week, Dr Thomas asks Lauren to help answer the phones. Lauren does not mind helping, but she finds that by the end of the fourth day, she has spent most of her time answering phones at reception. Lauren has only briefly observed Dr Thomas with patients or discussed professional issues with him.

How **appropriate** are each of the following responses by **Lauren** in this situation?

19A) Email the academic tutor supervising her attachment to share her concerns.
Answer:

    A. A very appropriate thing to do
    B. Appropriate but not ideal
    C. Inappropriate but not awful
    D. A very inappropriate thing to do

19B) Keep answering the phones without mentioning that the task does not seem to be connected to her professional development.
Answer:

    A. A very appropriate thing to do
    B. Appropriate but not ideal
    C. Inappropriate but not awful
    D. A very inappropriate thing to do

19C) Find a moment to speak privately with Dr Thomas and raise her concerns about the attachment.
Answer:

    A. A very appropriate thing to do
    B. Appropriate but not ideal
    C. Inappropriate but not awful
    D. A very inappropriate thing to do

20. A pharmacy student, Penny, is shadowing a junior pharmacist who confides that he thinks his long-term arthritic problems are due to the vaccine he had seven months ago. The junior pharmacist states that he has no evidence for this, but just has a gut feeling that the vaccine is not worth all the problems it causes. Penny is not sure how to respond to the junior pharmacist's claims, given that the vaccine is required for all pharmacists and pharmacy students.

How **appropriate** are each of the following responses by **Penny** in this situation?

20A) Ask if the junior pharmacist says this to his patients when discussing the vaccine.
Answer:

    A. A very appropriate thing to do
    B. Appropriate but not ideal
    C. Inappropriate but not awful
    D. A very inappropriate thing to do

20B) Ask the junior pharmacist if he would recommend any research papers on the topic.
Answer:

    A. A very appropriate thing to do
    B. Appropriate but not ideal
    C. Inappropriate but not awful
    D. A very inappropriate thing to do

21. A student, Sheetal, needs to see her GP but has had to rearrange the GP appointment twice to accommodate last-minute changes to her normal one-to-one meeting with her university tutor. Sheetal receives an email from her tutor stating that their next meeting will have to be changed to the exact same time as Sheetal's GP appointment. Sheetal knows that the next available GP appointment will not be for at least two weeks.

How **appropriate** are each of the following responses by **Sheetal** in this situation?

21A) Tell her tutor that she cannot reschedule the GP appointment again.
Answer:
      A.   A very appropriate thing to do
      B.   Appropriate but not ideal
      C.   Inappropriate but not awful
      D.   A very inappropriate thing to do

21B) Phone the GP and rearrange the appointment for the next available slot
Answer:
      A.   A very appropriate thing to do
      B.   Appropriate but not ideal
      C.   Inappropriate but not awful
      D.   A very inappropriate thing to do

22. Syon and Jamal have been assigned a joint research project by their academic university tutor. During the initial meeting, Jamal explains that he has been very busy preparing for a sporting event that he will be participating in one week from now. Jamal asks Syon if she is willing to do all the work in the next week since his time is limited. Syon is not sure how to respond. Syon thinks Jamal's proposal is unfair since the research represents most of their work on the project, and all the research will

have to be completed in the next few days for them to complete the project on time.

Choose **both** the **most appropriate** action and the **least appropriate** action that **Syon** should take in response to this situation. You will not receive any marks for this question unless you select **both** the most and least appropriate actions.

22A) Encourage Jamal to find an alternative arrangement so he can contribute equally to the research.
   A) **Most appropriate**
   B) **Least appropriate**

22B) Agree to work alone to complete the research if Jamal will agree to work alone to write up their report
   A) **Most appropriate**
   B) **Least appropriate**

23. Two pharmacy students, Gerry and Carmen, are interviewing a patient as part of a medication history on a hospital ward as part of their placement. The patient asks if the new medication he has just started taking will improve his prognosis. Carmen responds that the medication is very effective and states that the patient has every reason to be optimistic. The patient smiles and appears to be relieved to hear Carmen's comments. Gerry is concerned that Carmen's comments may have misled the patient to think the medication could cure his terminal condition, which Gerry knows the consultant has recently told the patient has spread. The consultant previously told Gerry and Carmen that the medication is not a cure but intended to improve the patient's quality of life in his final weeks.

Choose **both** the **most appropriate** action and the **least appropriate** action that **Gerry** should take in response to this situation.

23A) Clarify that the new medication improves the quality of life but cannot cure the patient's condition.
   A) **Most appropriate**
   B) **Least appropriate**

23B) Tell the patient that Carmen's comments are misleading and that he should not have false hope.
   A) **Most appropriate**
   B) **Least appropriate**

24. Sarah, a junior pharmacist, is working with another junior pharmacist, Michael, on the same ward. In the week that they have been working together, Sarah has noticed that Michael often arrives late at work and leaves very early. Sarah also feels as though Michael's mind seems elsewhere during the working day. Michael often needs Sarah to remind him about tasks he needs to complete. Choose **both** the **most appropriate** action and the **least appropriate** action that **Sarah** should take in response to this situation.

24A) Ask Michael if anything is impacting his ability to work.
   A) **Most appropriate**
   B) **Least appropriate**

24B) Keep a written record of the times when Michael arrives late or leaves early.
   A) **Most appropriate**
   B) **Least appropriate**

25. Monica is a pharmacy student who is on placement at a community pharmacy for a week. A superintendent pharmacist confides in Monica that pharmacy supplies/stock keep going missing from the storeroom; it is unclear whether someone is stealing the supplies or if

they have been misplaced. On the final day of her placement, Monica sees a dispenser zipping up her backpack as she exits the storeroom. The dispenser looks nervously from side to side, but does not appear to see Monica, who is at the far end of the corridor.

Choose **both** the **most appropriate** action and the **least appropriate** action that **Monica** should take in response to this situation.

25A) Notify her supervisor at the pharmacy about what she saw.
   A) **Most appropriate**
   B) **Least appropriate**

25B) Check the storeroom inventory to see if she can figure out what the dispenser might have taken
   A) **Most appropriate**
   B) **Least appropriate**

Section 2
Clinical Pharmacy, Law, and Ethics Questions

1. Which of the following is an incorrect statement?
   A. Pharmacists can issue an advanced supply of EHC
   B. Children under the age of 13 can consent to sexual activity
   C. The law is not intended to prosecute mutually agreed sexual activity
   D. The pharmacist can provide contraception to children under the age of 16 years OTC
   E. Ulipristal acetate can be supplied to a 14-year-old female as EHC

2. Which of the following sales are you allowed to make OTC?
   A. Sell 4 packs of 32x GR aspirin tablets
   B. Sell 200x effervescent 500mg paracetamol tablets
   C. Sell 500ml of a paracetamol 250mg/5ml solution
   D. Sell 32x (60mg pseudoephedrine) tablets incorrectly can only sell 720mg max
   E. Sell 2 packs of 100x 75mg aspirin tablets

3. Which of the following statement is correct?
   A. Any pack of medication with more than 32 tablets/capsules containing codeine/dihydrocodeine is classed as a POM
   B. Any pack of medication that contains more than 16 tablets/capsules containing paracetamol is classed as a POM
   C. Any pack of medication with more than 320mg of pseudoephedrine is classed as a POM

D. Any pack of medication with more than 108mg of ephedrine is classed as a POM

E. A pack of 28 duloxetine 30mg tablets can be sold OTC

4. Which of the following is not a legal component required on a prescription for it to be legally valid to dispense against?
A. Address of the prescriber
B. Patients address
C. Signature of the prescriber
D. Advanced electronic signature – for authorisation of electronic prescriptions
E. Age of the patient if under 18 years

5. You receive a prescription written on a particular type of RX form. Which of the following is most likely to be repeatable again?
A. FP10
B. Private
C. FP10 MDA
D. Emergency supply over fax, then fulfilled by a GP10 form
E. WP10

6. You receive a private prescription request to dispense one item. The prescription also stated that it can be repeated 3 times. Which of the following prescription items can you repeatedly dispense 3 times from the same RX form?
A. Morphine 10mg/1ml solution for injection 10 ampoules
B. Buprenorphine 5mcg/hr 2 patches
C. Morphine 10mg/5ml 100ml oral solution
D. Shortec ® 5 mg 56 capsules
E. Methadone 1mg/ml oral solution 20mL

7. You receive a prescription to dispense 28x dihydrocodeine tartrate 120 mg tablets for a patient, which of the following is correct?
   A. As this drug is a schedule 4 CD, it must be dispensed within 6 months of the date on the prescription.
   B. As this drug is a schedule 5 CD, it must be dispensed within 6 months of the date on the prescription.
   C. As this drug is a schedule 2 CD, it must be dispensed within 28 days of the date on the prescription.
   D. As this drug is not a controlled drug, the RX is valid for 12 months.
   E. As this drug is a schedule 5 CD, it must be dispensed within 28 days of the date on the prescription.

8. You are clearing out old, archived files from your pharmacy's stock room. Which of the following is correct regarding private prescriptions that have previously been dispensed?
   A. Private prescriptions must be kept for 2 years from the date of supply
   B. Private repeatable prescriptions must be kept for 24 months after the initial supply is made against the prescription
   C. Private prescriptions must be kept for 5 years from the date of supply
   D. Private prescriptions must be sent to the NHSBSA for processing
   E. Private repeatable prescriptions must be kept for 12 months after the final supply is made against the prescription

9. Mr FT has recently been released from prison and brings you an FP10 NHS prescription requesting for you to dispense the following:

  - 56x sertraline 50mg tablets - One to be taken daily
  - 56x sertraline 100mg tablets - One to be taken daily
  - 200x 30mg/500mg co-codamol tablets - PRN
  - 56x amlodipine 5mg tablets - One to be taken daily

The prescription also stated the following:

- The prescription was dated 13/05/22 and today is 15/05/22
- The patient's DOB: is 14/04/1988
- The patient's address: HMP
- The prescriber's registration number was 23CV45BN

Which of the following should you do once you have handed the prescription to the patient?

  A. Charge the patient 4 RX charges to cover the POM supply
  B. Charge the patient 3 RX charges to cover the POM supply.
  C. Charge the patient 2 RX charges to cover the POM supply.
  D. Charge the patient 1 RX charge to cover the POM supply.
  E. Charge the patient no RX charges to cover the POM supply.

10. You are working in a remote village today and a patient comes in to get their prescription. The RX is presented on an 'FMed 296 prescription form'. Which of the following describes this prescription?
    A. Private CD prescription
    B. Veterinary prescription
    C. Military prescription
    D. NHS hospital prescription
    E. Tertiary care prescription

11. Which of the following prescription can you not dispense at your community pharmacy?
    A. Morphine 10 MR capsules from an FP10 form
    B. Methadone 1mg/1ml from an FP10MDA form
    C. Fentanyl 12mcg/hr patches from an FMed 296 form
    D. Methylphenidate 28mg MR capsules from an FP10PCD form
    E. Codeine 30mg tablets from an FMed 296 form

12. You are going through the dispensing SOP with a new colleague you are training in your pharmacy. Soon they will also begin to dispense prescriptions. Which of the following is true about dispensing?
    A. It is a legal requirement to place the dispensing label on the actual container such as the bottle/inhaler/tub rather than the outer container.
    B. It is a legal requirement to place the dispensing label on the outer container such as the bottle/inhaler/tub rather than the actual container.

C. It is a legal requirement to place the dispensing labels on the actual device/inner packaging such as the bottle/inhaler/tub and on the outer container.
D. It is recommended to place dispensing labels on the actual container such as the bottle/inhaler/tub rather than the outer container.
E. Dispensing labels legally need to state the patient's date of birth.

13. Parenteral POM medications can be administered in emergency life-threatening situations for the benefit of the patient to save a life. An example of this can be the administration of adrenaline when a patient is experiencing an anaphylactic shock. Which of the following is this stipulated in?
   A. Schedule 4 of The Misuse of Drugs Act 1971
   B. Schedule 21 of The Medicines (Pharmacies) (Responsible Pharmacist) Regulations 2008
   C. Schedule 19 of the Human Medicines Regulations 2012
   D. The National Health Service Act 2006
   E. This is not governed by any regulation

14. Which of the following is not an exemption by which you may supply a POM without a prescription?
   A. PSD
   B. PGD
   C. Emergency Supply
   D. The occupational therapist signed order
   E. The pharmacist signed order

15. You are carrying out a training session with pharmacy students about supplying emergency supplies of medication. You explain that the smallest quantity available should be supplied. Which of the following would be most appropriate to supply as an emergency supply?
    A. 5 tablets of potassium bromide
    B. 100g of hydrocortisone 1% cream
    C. 24x tablets of naproxen 500mg tablets
    D. 1 OP Salbutamol CFC Free MDI inhaler
    E. 30g of clobetasone butyrate 0.05% cream

16. Under regulation 225 of the HMR 2012, which of the following is legally required by the pharmacist when making an emergency supply of medication at a patient's request?
    A. Interview the patient/representative to make an informed decision.
    B. Interview the patient's prescriber to make an informed decision.
    C. Ensure a prescription is received from the prescriber after the emergency supply is made.
    D. A prescription must be issued within 62 hours of the emergency supply.
    E. Do not supply any type of controlled drug as an emergency supply.

17. In England, the CPCS is an?
    A. Essential service
    B. Enhanced service
    C. Advanced service
    D. Nationally recognised PGD
    E. Private referral Service

18. A signed order is not an order; however, it is still classed as a legal document when supplying POM medications with it. How long should a signed order be kept, after supply?
    A. 6 months
    B. 12 months
    C. 18 months
    D. 24 months
    E. 48 months

19. Drug X is a prescription-only medication. However, now healthcare staff who work in a drug-related service by legislation 'Human Medicines (Amendment) (no.3) Regulations 2015, permitted to administer it to patients without a prescription or PGD/PSD. What is drug X?
    A. Naltrexone
    B. Naloxone
    C. Naproxen
    D. Nebivolol
    E. Nicardipine

20. The pregnancy prevention program (PPP) was introduced to prevent pregnancies. Which of the statement best describes the purpose of the PPP?
    A. To provide free EHC for all females who have unprotected intercourse and want to prevent an unplanned pregnancy.
    B. To provide males with adequate barrier methods of contraception through the C card scheme.
    C. To offer walk-in sexual health clinics in each locality to control pregnancy rates.
    D. To ensure that females of childbearing age that take teratogenic medication and are

also on adequate contraception to prevent pregnancy.

E. To offer females of childbearing age EHC for free, especially those who are taking teratogenic medication.

21. You are handing out a prescription for 56x alitretinoin 30mg capsules for Miss JB. The directions advise the patient to take 1 capsule daily. You are careful when handing out this medication as it is a very expensive prescription item. Which of the following piece of advice must be given to the patient during the hand-out?

A. To take the medication at the same time on each date
B. Ensure to take adequate contraception while on this medication
C. Ensure you take the medicine while sitting upright, with a glass of water
D. Take this medication with food
E. The patient must get her serum vitamin A levels checked within 3 months of treatment

22. The pregnancy prevention program applies restrictions to prescriptions for specific drugs. When drug ABC is prescribed for women, the treatment period should only be limited to 30 days and once the prescription is issued by the prescriber, it is only valid for 7 days, which it must be dispensed within. Which of the following drug is covered under the pregnancy prevention program?

A. Morphine 10mg/5ml oral solution
B. Nitrofurantoin 100mg MR capsules
C. Lamotrigine 50mg tablets
D. Labetalol 200mg tablets
E. Isotretinoin 10mg capsules

23. Miss AP has come to you asking for advice, she tells you that she has epilepsy and has been seizure free for the last 5 years while being stable on sodium valproate. However, she has not had her period for the last two months and has done a pregnancy test this morning to find that it was positive. What should you advise her?

A. Advise her to stop taking the sodium valproate from today and signpost her to her GP immediately.

B. Signpost her to the nearest urgent care centre immediately.

C. Advise her to continue taking her sodium valproate as directed by the doctor. However, she must arrange to discuss this with her prescriber at the earliest instance.

D. Advise her to continue taking her sodium valproate as directed by the doctor. Valproate only enters the placenta in the third trimester, so that is when she should lower her dose.

E. She does not need to change anything with her current treatment regimen.

24. You receive a call from your veterinary surgeon asking for an emergency supply to be made at the prescriber's request for an animal they are treating. How do you respond?

A. Make the emergency supply, if you can retrieve a prescription from the veterinary surgeon within 72 hours

B. You do not make the emergency supply and request a prescription to be sent for a supply to be made

C. Make the emergency supply at the prescriber's request

D. Refuse to make the supply and signpost to the nearest out-of-hours service
E. Tell them you do not deal with veterinary matters and signpost to the nearest chemist

25. Which of the following prescriber cannot prescribe a schedule 2 controlled drug?
    A. Pharmacist independent prescriber
    B. Medical doctors registered with the GMC
    C. Dentists registered with the GDC
    D. Veterinary surgeon registered with the RCVS
    E. Optometrist independent prescriber

26. You receive a prescription to be dispensed from a physiotherapist-independent prescriber. You are requested to dispense a controlled drug. Which of the following are you allowed to dispense from this prescription?
    A. Fentanyl 12mcg/hr patches
    B. Methadone 1mg/1ml oral solution
    C. Morphine suppository
    D. Buprenorphine 20mcg/hr patches
    E. Diamorphine 5mg powder for injection

27. Your trainee pharmacist is preparing for their registration exam and ask you about the prescribing scope of podiatrist independent prescribers. Which of the following can be prescribed by a podiatrist?
    A. Buprenorphine 5 mcg/hr patches
    B. Diazepam 5mg tablets
    C. Morphine 10mg MR capsules
    D. Oxycodone 1mg/1ml solution
    E. Brinzolamide 10mg/ml eye drops solution

28. A prescription is presented to you requesting to dispense lisdexamfetamine 20mg MR capsules. Which of the following prescribers can issue this prescription in the UK?
   A. A Swiss-registered and approved prescriber
   B. Community nurse practitioner prescriber
   C. Therapeutic radiographer independent prescriber
   D. Chiropodist Independent Prescriber
   E. Nurse independent prescriber

29. You are checking the registration details of a prescriber to ensure that the prescription you have received is valid. You are trying to confirm the details on the 'Health and Care Professions Council'. Which of the following professional would not be registered with this registration body?
   A. Optometrists
   B. Orthoptists
   C. Physiotherapists
   D. Paramedics
   E. Radiographers

30. Which of the following regulatory bodies are responsible for overseeing and enforcing safety of wholesale distribution of medicines?
   A. MHRA
   B. NHS digital
   C. GPhC
   D. NHS England
   E. Health watch

31. When a signed order is supplied from a healthcare professional for a POM supply to a registered pharmacy, which of the following must be done?
    A. The signed order must be retained for 5 years
    B. An entry must be made in the private POM register
    C. The signed order must be retained for no longer than a year
    D. The signed order must be patient-specific
    E. A signed order must be on an appropriately headed NHS form.

32. What is not a legal category of veterinary medicines in the UK?
    A. POM-V
    B. POM-VPS
    C. NFA-GSL
    D. AVM-GSL
    E. POM-P

33. What does SAES Stand for in the pharmaceutical industry?
    A. Small Animal Exemption Schemes
    B. Saving Animals Extinct Species
    C. Special Assistant for Environmental Services
    D. State Agricultural Experiment station
    E. Species-Specific Authorising Exemption Services

34. Which of the following is false about the legal requirements of vet prescriptions for medications prescribed under the veterinary cascade?

A. The name and address of the pet's owner are required on the prescription
B. The species of the animal is a requirement on the prescription
C. The animal's date of birth is not a legal prescription requirement
D. The veterinary prescriber must state their RCVS registration number when prescribing schedule 4 controlled drugs
E. For a repeatable prescription, it must state specifically how many times the prescription can be repeated.

35. Veterinary prescriptions written by appropriate practitioners do not need to be on standardised forms like human prescription medications. However, for certain drugs, the following statement needs to be written, 'prescribed for the treatment of an animal or herd under my care'. Which of the following does this apply to?
A. All POM drugs
B. Schedule 2 drugs only
C. Schedule 2 and 3 drugs only
D. Schedule 3 drugs only
E. Schedule 2-5 controlled drugs

36. You are sorting out archives of prescriptions and records. Which of the following statement about record keeping requirements is false?
A. Veterinary prescriptions should be kept for 5 years
B. Private prescriptions for schedule 2 and 3 controlled drugs must be submitted to the NHSBSA for processing
C. Veterinary prescriptions must be submitted to the NHSBSA for processing

D. Schedule 2 drug prescriptions should not exceed more than 30 days of treatment unless there is a justifiable reason
E. Veterinary prescriptions should not be returned to the veterinary prescriber

37. All POM medications in the UK usually have a marketing authorisation license for human use. It is considered unlawful to prescribe such an item for veterinary use on a veterinary prescription. Which of the following would prevent such a supply for a canine animal from being unlawful?
A. To prescribe on an FP10SS form
B. To prescribe on a veterinary prescription, the prescriber must state 'for administration under the cascade'.
C. To be prescribed on a private prescription form
D. You cannot use medications licensed for human use in animals
E. Prescription requiring off-license use of POM medications requires a license from the home office

38. When prescribing medications for veterinary use under the cascade. Which of the following are not required on the dispensed label of a veterinary medication?
A. The name of the prescribing veterinary surgeon
B. The species of the animal
C. Appropriate dosage directed by the prescriber
D. The words 'for animal treatment only'
E. The pharmacist's registration number

39. How long should veterinary requisition forms be retained?
    A. They do not need to be retained
    B. 6 months
    C. 12 months
    D. 24 months
    E. 60 months

40. A 14-year-old female is asking to purchase an emergency contraceptive pill for herself. You take her to the consulting room for a private consultation. She tells you that the intercourse took place earlier in the day with her long-term partner, however, the condom broke and is worried about pregnancy. You are also informed that she has taken an emergency contraceptive pill earlier this month. Which of the following statement is incorrect?
    A. Ulipristal acetate cannot be used as EHC more than once in the same cycle
    B. Ulipristal acetate and levonorgestrel may be used together in the same cycle
    C. Levonorgestrel can be used as EHC more than once in the same cycle
    D. Levonorgestrel 1500mg is the licensed dose to supply as EHC over the counter
    E. Ulipristal acetate and levonorgestrel should not be used concomitantly

41. Organisations who handle and deal with controlled drugs must have appropriate standard operating procedures and protocols in place when handling CD medications. Also, an accountable officer must be nominated. Which of the following regulation is this governed by?
    A. The HMR 2012
    B. The Health Act 2006
    C. The Misuse of Drugs Act 1971
    D. The NHS Act 2006
    E. The Accounting Officer Act 1995

42. A female has come into your pharmacy with a requisition form requesting fentanyl® patches to be supplied against it. Which of the following would this be written on for an appropriate supply in England?
    A. GP10A
    B. CDRF
    C. WP10CDF
    D. FP10PCD
    E. FP10CDF

43. Which of the following statements regarding supplies of schedule 2 and 3 controlled drugs against requisition forms in England is false?
    A. A photocopied requisition form is not valid to supply against
    B. In emergency situations, doctors and dentists can be provided with schedule 2 controlled drugs if they supply a requisition form within 24 hours of the supply
    C. It is classed as good practice to keep a copy of the requisition for 2 years after the supply
    D. The requisition form must be sent to the NHS processing body
    E. In emergency situations, doctors and dentists can be provided with schedule 2 or 3 controlled drugs if they supply a requisition form within 72 hours of the supply

44. Midwife supply order cannot obtain which of the following CD?
    A. Diamorphine
    B. Methadone
    C. Morphine
    D. Heroin
    E. pethidine

45. Which of the following is not legally required for a midwife supply order to be valid and to supply against?
    A. The total quantity of the drug being requested
    B. The name of the patient who will be administered the CD
    C. Name of the midwife
    D. Registration number of the midwife
    E. Signature of an appropriate medical officer

46. You receive a prescription requesting you to dispense a schedule 2 controlled drug. Which of the following would you be able to dispense?
    A. RX states 'to dispense 28x Twenty-eight morphine sulphate M/R tablets', to Take one daily.
    B. RX states 'to dispense 56x Fifty-Six oxycodone 5mg five-milligram tablets', to Take One tablet TWICE daily.
    C. RX states 'to dispense 28x Twenty-eight morphine sulphate 100mg one-hundred-milligram tablets', to Take daily as directed.
    D. RX states 'to dispense 58x Fifty-Six oxycodone 5mg five-milligram tablets', to Take One tablet TWICE daily.
    E. RX states 'to dispense 28x Twenty-eight morphine sulphate 10mg ten-milligram I/R tablets', to Take two daily as per GP.

47. Which of the following statement is true?
    A. It is a legal requirement that the maximum quantity of schedule 2, 3 and 4 CDs prescribed should not exceed 28 days of treatment on a prescription.
    B. It is a legal requirement that the maximum quantity of schedule 2, 3, 4 and 5 CDs

prescribed should not exceed 30 days of treatment on a prescription.

C. It is a legal requirement that the maximum quantity of schedule 2, 3, 4 and 5 CDs prescribed should not exceed 28 days of treatment on a prescription.

D. It is a recommendation that the maximum quantity of schedule 2, 3 and 4 CDs prescribed should not exceed 28 days of treatment on a prescription.

E. It is a recommendation that the maximum quantity of schedule 2, 3 and 4 CDs prescribed should not exceed 30 days of treatment on a prescription.

48. Which of the following dose instruction would legally be accepted on an NHS prescription for dexamphetamine 10mg tablets?
   A. Twice daily as directed
   B. When required as per the neurologist
   C. Four tablets to be given every hourly as directed by the doctor. Can increase according to the response
   D. Take One Daily when required for anxiety
   E. Take One as per the titration regimen

49. Your trainee pharmacy technician has never seen a methadone instalment prescription. Which of the following statement is accurate about instalment prescription?
   A. Instalment prescriptions allow to dispense the total quantity of drug stated on the prescription in separate instalments over several days. The first instalment must be dispensed within 28 days of the prescription issue date. The remainder of the instalment can run beyond the 28-day limit.

B. Instalment prescriptions allow dispensing of controlled drugs several times within a 7-day period. Usually used to manage opioid dependence. The first instalment must be dispensed within 28 days of the prescription issue date. The remainder of the instalment can run beyond the 28-day limit.

C. Instalment prescriptions allow dispensing the total quantity of the drug stated on the prescription in separate instalments over several days. The first instalment must be dispensed within 7 days of the prescription issue date. The remainder of the instalment can run beyond the 28-day limit.

D. Instalment prescriptions allow dispensing the total quantity of the drug stated on the prescription in separate instalments over several days. The first instalment must be dispensed within 28 days of the prescription issue date. The remainder of the instalment cannot run beyond the 28-day limit.

E. Instalment prescriptions allow dispensing the total quantity of the drug stated on the prescription in separate instalments over several days. The first instalment must be dispensed within 28 days of the prescription issue date. The remainder of the instalment cannot run beyond the 30-day limit.

50. Mr JK is a 32-year-old male who comes into your pharmacy daily for his supervised methadone consumption. You have received a new instalment prescription for his next methadone supply, this prescription starts on the 16/08/2023 and finishes on the 22/08/2023. This new prescription starts today, and you

check that Mr JK has collected all his previous methadone instalments including yesterday. A few days later, you realise that Mr JK has not turned up at your pharmacy since 16/08/2023 and today is 20/08/2023. What should you do?

A. Contact Mr JK and inform him that his methadone CD prescription is about to run out and that he needs to quickly come to you to collect the remainder of his instalments

B. Report Mr JK to the CDAO for failing to collect his instalments prescription

C. Contact Mr JK's Keyworker/prescriber from the drug clinic that he has missed more than 3 doses and that this prescription is now void

D. Supply all the missed instalments to Mr JK

E. Wait until Mr JK contacts your pharmacy

51. Which of the following statement about the safe custody of controlled drugs is false?

A. Patient-returned CDs need to be kept in the CD cabinet and separated from regular stock until they are destroyed

B. Expired CDs need to be kept in the CD cabinet and separated from regular stock until they are destroyed

C. All schedule 2 controlled drugs require safe custody

D. Buprenorphine sublingual tablets are exempt from safe custody

E. CD medications when out of the CD cabinet, must be under the direct supervision of the pharmacist

52. What is the T28 exemption?
    A. An exemption issued by the environmental agency that allows pharmacies to sort and dispose of CDs. To comply with the 2001 regulations, these CDs must be denatured prior to disposal.
    B. An exemption issued by the NHS BSA for medically exempt patients from paying a prescription charge.
    C. This exemption is only issued to a hospital pharmacy dispensary
    D. Allows you to treat certain waste at water treatment works to reduce the volume for transport, or to make it easier to handle waste recovery
    E. This exemption allows pharmacists to prescribe for minor ailments.

53. Today at your community pharmacy, you have an authorised witness to help you destroy unwanted CD drugs from the CD cabinet. Which of the following is false?
    A. An authorised witness is required to denature and destroy the patient returned schedule 2, 3 and 4 (part-1) controlled drugs.
    B. An authorised witness is required to denature and destroy expired, obsolete, unwanted schedule 2, 3, and 4 (part-1) controlled drugs.
    C. You are required to make an entry in the controlled drugs register when you destroy schedule 2 controlled drugs.
    D. You are not required to make an entry in the controlled drugs register when you destroy patient returned schedule 2, 3 and 4 (part-1) controlled drugs.
    E. Schedule 4 part 2 drugs do not need to be denatured.

54. Which of the following does not require record keeping?
    A. Methylphenidate 10mg tablets
    B. Morphine 5mg capsules
    C. Sativex Oro-mucosal spray
    D. Fentanyl 25mcg/hr patches
    E. Dexamethasone 500mcg tablets

55. You have just supplied Oxycodone oral solution 5mg/5ml, 250ml to Mrs WP. Which of the following piece of information is NOT legally required as part of the CD Entry?
    A. Date of the prescription issue
    B. Name of the patient
    C. Quantity of the drug supplied
    D. Address of the patient
    E. Details of the prescriber/licence holder

56. Controlled drug entries in the register must comply with which of the following?
    A. Must be computerized
    B. Entered within 72hours of the CD supply
    C. Entered in chronological order
    D. Have an authorized witness countersign
    E. Entries can be amendable/cancelled later

57. Your pharmacy assistant is date-checking medicinal stock in gallery two of your dispensary. She finds 17 original packs of 32x paracetamol 500mg tablets which have an expiration date of 10/24. This is approximately 3 months from today. She comes to you asking for advice. Which of the following is NOT the best course of action to take?
    A. Destroy all 17 packs of paracetamol and place them in the medication dupe bin

B. Rotate stock and ensure these packets are used first, add short-dated stickers to it
C. Place some of the short-dated packets with the Pharmacy-Only medications and sell the packets OTC
D. Make a record of the short, dated boxes in your stock register
E. Ensure the integrity of each packet is maintained and advice that these paracetamol tablets can safely be consumed till the end of October.

58. You are carrying out a session for trainee pharmacists. Which of the following phrase is an example of person-centred healthcare?
A. Stop taking any over-the-counter vitamins
B. Hello, my name is Amit. I am the pharmacist and shall be reviewing your medications today
C. Give me your medication list, as I need to quickly go through them
D. This appointment slot is only 10 minutes only
E. You will have to take tablets

59. How can a healthcare professional be culturally informed?
A. Ask open questions
B. Assume all females have long hair
C. Have a rigid structure for consultations
D. Assume anyone under the age of 16 years requires consent from their parent/guardian
E. Arrange a translator for every BAME patient consultation

60. Every sector, industry or workplace has a culture. What is meant by the term punitive culture?
    A. Assigning blame and punishment to individuals within a team
    B. Balancing accountability across the team to improve patient safety
    C. Having a no-blame policy
    D. Conveying a culture of no fear/openness
    E. Learning from mistakes

61. Which of the following is not part of the 'RPS error reporting standards'?
    A. To report the error
    B. To share what was learnt from the error
    C. To act to improve systems
    D. To be open honest
    E. To ensure colleagues do not make the same mistakes again

62. What does NRLS Stand for?
    A. National Rise in Living Standards
    B. National Reporting and Learning system
    C. Native Review of Learning Systems
    D. Notice Rate of Long Studies
    E. National Review of Latent Standards

63. Which of the following is not a direct sign of abuse or neglect?
    A. Fractures
    B. Dirty clothes
    C. Behavioural problem
    D. STI
    E. Cough

64. Miss ML, an 11-year-old female, has come in to confide with a member of staff at your pharmacy. She tells you that she has had sexual intercourse with her boyfriend and is worried about pregnancy. Which of the following is true?
    A. It is a criminal offence for persons under 13 years of age to be involved in sexual acts
    B. It is a criminal offence for persons under 17 years of age to be involved in sexual acts.
    C. Females aged between 10-13 years cannot get pregnant
    D. It is a criminal offence for persons under 18 years of age to be involved in sexual acts
    E. Females aged between 10-13 years who have consensual sex can have ulipristal acetate as emergency contraception OTC

65. Today you are working in your local community pharmacy as a locum pharmacist. A 13-year-old female has come to get emergency contraception. Which of the following is not part of the Fraser guidelines?
    A. The young patient must have sufficient maturity and intelligence about EHC
    B. The treatment must be in the best interest of the young patient
    C. The patient's physical or mental health will suffer if an appropriate supply is not given
    D. The young patient is likely to have intercourse with or without contraception
    E. You must tell her parent or guardian

66. Which of the following is most likely a sign of sexual abuse?
    A. Repeated EHC supply
    B. Bruise on arms
    C. Debt
    D. Dirty lingerie
    E. Genital mutilation

67. You are carrying out a domiciliary visit to Mr JL's residential home on behalf of your primary care network. Upon carrying out a medication review, you suspect financial abuse of this vulnerable adult and would like to report this to the relevant body such as social services / designated care workers. You are unsure of Mr JL's mental capacity, how would you respond?
    A. Carry out an investigation with the alleged perpetrator.
    B. Take immediate action by reporting this case to social services.
    C. Contact Mr JL's GP, seeking advice from them about his capacity.
    D. Signpost the patient to get counselling.
    E. When documenting on the patient's record, to make notes of the encounter. Only report when allowed to do so by Mr JL.

68. Which of the following is not a part of medicines optimization?
    A. Understand the patient's experience with their medication.
    B. Evidence-based choice of medication/regimen.
    C. Aim to deprescribe medication.
    D. Ensure medicine usage is safe and appropriate.
    E. Make medicines optimization part of routine practice.

69. You are participating in an outreach session for medicines management for the 'Intercalated Care Board' today. You are explaining the need for legal storage requirements of certain medications within a dispensary setting and its importance to complying with regulations. The Medicines Act 1968 regulates the authorization, sale, and supply of medicines. Which of the following legislation consolidates most part of the Medicines Act 1968?
   A. The Food and Drug Act 1985
   B. The Human Medicines Act 2002
   C. The NHS Act 2004
   D. The Human Medicines Regulation 2012
   E. The Medicines Act 2023 (revised regulations)

70. Which of the following legislation covers the manufacturing, prescribing, sale and supply of medication to animals in the UK?
   A. The Veterinary Medicines Regulation 2013
   B. The Human Medicines Regulation 2012
   C. The Animal Welfare Act 2006
   D. The Welfare of Farmed Animals (England) Regulations 2007
   E. The Medicine for Veterinary Use Act 2008

71. Your pharmacy premises is located within a large food supermarket. Which of the following is incorrect about GSL medicines?
   A. GSL medication can be purchased in the supermarket
   B. GSL medications cannot be sold in the absence of a pharmacist
   C. GSL medicines have different product licenses to P-only medicines
   D. Aspirin can be sold as a GSL medication
   E. GSL medication can be formulated in powder form for oral use

72. You are sorting out the delivery of medications that came into your pharmacy this morning. You segregate pharmacy-only medications from POM medications. Which of the following could be a P medication?
    A. Naproxen 250mg tablets
    B. Promazine 25mg tablets
    C. Salbutamol Nebules
    D. Lansoprazole 30mg capsules
    E. Folic acid 5mg tablet

73. You are asked to make an OTC Sale of orlistat for a patient, which of the following is appropriate to sell?
    A. Orlistat 240mg tablets (pack of 56 tablets)
    B. Orlistat 180mg tablets (pack of 84 tablets)
    C. Orlistat 120mg tablets (pack of 56 tablets)
    D. Orlistat 60mg tablets (pack of 84 tablets)
    E. Orlistat 30mg tablets (pack of 56 tablets)

74. Your trainee pharmacist whom you are working with today asks you why pseudoephedrine has controlled limits of sale and supply OTC. Which of the following is a reason why pseudoephedrine has the potential to be misused?
    A. It has a potential for misuse in the illicit production of methylamphetamine
    B. When taken more than 30mg/dose it can cause hypotensive effects in the patient
    C. It has a potential for misuse in the illicit production of morphine sulphate
    D. It causes oligospermia
    E. It has a potential for misuse in the illicit production of lisdexamphetamine

75. Which of the following is not a sign of possible drug misuse?
    A. Lack of symptoms
    B. Rehearsed answers
    C. Impatient behaviour
    D. Opportunistic behaviour
    E. Infrequent requests for drug

76. You have just received your morning delivery from the wholesaler, who has brought a bag of medication to you. You receive this delivery and sign for it. You sort out the medications out of the bag in alphabetical order. Which of the following drug would require safe custody in a controlled drugs cupboard?
    A. Phenobarbital 60mg tablets
    B. Zolpidem® 10mg tablets
    C. Buprenorphine 5mcg/hr patches
    D. Midazolam 5mg/5ml solution for injection
    E. Tramadol 100mg MR capsules

77. You have received an instalment prescription for Mr FG. The prescription is asking to dispense Physeptone solution sugar-free 1mg/1ml, for a total quantity of 490ml over 2 weeks. The prescription starts on the 24th of May till the 6th of June. Mr FG is to receive a daily dose of 35ml. Today is the 26th of May and Mr FG has missed all previous doses from the 24th of May. Mr FG has come to collect his medication from you, what is the most appropriate course of action to take?
    A. Refuse the supply of Physeptone and void the prescription
    B. Supply the patient with 35ml of Physeptone
    C. Supply the patient with 105ml of Physeptone
    D. Ask the patient to get a new prescription
    E. Refer the patient back to the prescriber

78. Miss BM brings in an instalment prescription for Buprenorphine sublingual tablets as substitution therapy for her opioid dependence. She would like you to dispense her first instalment today so she could take it with her, she is patiently waiting. The date that the prescription was signed, which is recorded next to the prescriber's signature box states 01/6/23. Today is 30/06/23, which of the following statement best describes the action you should take?
    A. Dispense the first instalment for Miss BM and supervise her consumption
    B. Contact the prescriber issuing the prescription to query the supply
    C. Refuse the supply and report Miss BM to the CDAO
    D. Refuse the supply as the prescription has expired
    E. Ask the patient if she has been using illicit opioids

79. Your trainee pharmacist is asking about expiration dates of prescriptions, which of the following is incorrect about a prescription requesting to dispense morphine sulphate 10mg/5ml oral solution on an FP10 NHS prescription form?
    A. The prescription can be dispensed within 7 days of the issue date.
    B. The prescription can be dispensed within 28 days of the issue date.
    C. The prescription can be dispensed within 30 days of the issue date.
    D. The prescription must be dispensed within 6 months of the issue date.
    E. The prescription must be dispensed within 365 days of the issue date.

80. The dispenser asks you to deal with a prescription that has morphine on it. You see that the prescription is for morphine 10mg modified release tablets. The prescription has an issue date of 15/08/23 and today is 31/08/23. Can you dispense this prescription and supply it?
   A. Yes, you can fulfil this prescription as it is within the 30-day expiration period.
   B. Yes, you can fulfil this prescription as it is within the 28-day expiration period.
   C. Yes, you can fulfil this prescription as it is within the 60-day expiration period.
   D. Yes, you can fulfil this prescription as it is within the 180-day expiration period.
   E. No, you cannot fulfil this prescription as it has expired. The patient needs to get a new prescription issued.

81. Mr SD is asking your counter assistant to purchase 'Kaolin and Morphine Mixture BP' for himself. The counter assistant refuses the sale and informs the patient that he must get a prescription for it. The patient becomes infuriated by this and asks to speak with the pharmacist. How should you deal with this?
   A. Supply the patient with 'Kaolin and Morphine Mixture BP'.
   B. Tell the patient that he must get a prescription for it.
   C. Tell the patient to leave the premises and ban him from returning.
   D. Despite being stocked, lie to the patient, and tell him that you have not got any in stock.
   E. Signpost the patient to the nearest Urgent Care Centre, while refusing a supply.

82. Miss WR has come with her 1-year-old son to get a prescription fulfilled for him. The prescription is for amoxicillin 125mg/5ml oral solution, to dispense 100ml in total. You see that the issue date on the prescription is 22/12/2023, the prescription expires in 3 days' time, hence is still within the required time to dispense. Which of the following actions should you take?
   A. Refuse the supply as the prescription is almost 6 months old and about to expire.
   B. Refuse the supply as amoxicillin is no longer indicated for the patient.
   C. Ask Miss WR more about the indication she is giving the amoxicillin to her son before you supply it.
   D. Dispense the prescription for the patient.
   E. Dispense the prescription but advice that next time, she must fulfil prescriptions earlier.

83. A paper prescription is presented to you requiring to dispense oxycodone 10mg tablets. You return the prescription back to the patient to be amended by the prescriber as you are unable to dispense it legally. Which of the following could be a reason as to why the prescription needs amending?
   A. The directions state to take 1 tablet BD ASD
   B. The patient's title is missing from their name
   C. The prescriber did not write their full name
   D. The prescription is written in an FP10MDA script
   E. The total quantity of oxycodone is not written in words and figures

84. A young male in his early 20s has come in to purchase medication over the counter. He tells you that we would like to purchase 'Ovalumunpoly®' for his head. You question him further and find that he is from Brazil on holiday in the UK and has run out of his medication. You ask if he has any proof or evidence such packaging of the medication, but he, unfortunately, has not. You carry out some online research to find that the active ingredient in 'Ovalumunpoly®' is venlafaxine. You refuse the supply, and do which of the following?

   A. Refuse an OTC supply and tell him to go back to Brazil.
   B. Refuse an OTC supply but refer to a prescribing practitioner such as a private GP.
   C. Refuse the OTC supply but issue an emergency supply.
   D. Make an OTC supply of a UK-licensed product with the same/similar active ingredient(s).
   E. Sell the patient some diphenhydramine

85. Today you are leading a session with year 2 pharmacy students at your local university teaching them about the legalities around prescriptions, which of the following is not a necessary legal requirement of an NHS prescription?

   A. Prescribers signature
   B. Written in indelible ink
   C. Age of the patient if under 12 years
   D. Patients signature
   E. A valid date of when the prescription was issued

86. Miss PV has come to the counter at your pharmacy asking to purchase some chlorphenamine 2mg/5ml syrup. She tells you she is in a rush today and needs to quickly get it and go. You question her further to find out why she needs it and are informed that it has been recommended by the veterinary doctor for her dog's topical rash. How would you proceed with this?

    A. Sell her the chlorphenamine as it was recommended by a prescriber and is available OTC

    B. Sell her the chlorphenamine as it is licensed for veterinary use under a cascade

    C. Refuse the sale and signpost her to the nearest urgent care centre

    D. Refuse the sale because chlorphenamine is not licensed for veterinary use OTC

    E. Supply the chlorphenamine as an emergency supply to Miss PV for her dog and ask for a script to be supplied to fulfil the supply from a prescriber within 72hrs

87. Today is a Sunday and Mr SD has run out of his medication and took his last dose yesterday. He has come in asking to get his prescription for cinnarizine 15mg tablets. You look through your computer system and find that no prescriptions have been issued by his GP since the last supply, that he collected last month. Mr SD becomes very upset; he tells you that his vertigo gets worse if he does not take his dose and has not had any this morning? What is the best course of action to take?

    A. Tell Mr SD to order his prescriptions earlier and that it is his fault

    B. Sell a pack of cinnarizine 15mg tablets OTC

C. Refer him to the out-of-hours service for a prescription

D. Signpost Mr SD to the nearest pharmacy to get an emergency supply as you do not have a pack in the dispensary

E. There is nothing you can do; he must contact his GP tomorrow

88. You are approached by a customer asking to purchase a medication. He tells you that it begins with the letter 'B', he has the name written down on the piece of paper. He finds it difficult to pronounce the name and shows you the paper. It is for his mother, who has purchased it before and is on no other long-term medications. Which of the following could it NOT be?
A. Buccastem®
B. Buccolam®
C. Buscopan
D. Bisacodyl
E. Benzydamine hydrochloride

89. The trainee pharmacist is sorting out the afternoon delivery of medications that have just been delivered to your community pharmacy. She has become a little confused with them and asks for your help. She has stacked all the drugs on the countertop and would like to know which of them should be put into the CD cabinet. Which drug is it?
A. Dexamphetamine
B. Dexamethasone
C. Desmopressin
D. Dapsone
E. Donepezil

90. A nurse has come to your pharmacy to return a bag of old medications. You look through the bag and find that many of them are still unexpired and are a mixture of ampoules. The bag contains, 4x haloperidol 5mg/1ml ampoules, 11x water for injection ampoules, 2x glycopyrronium 200mcg/ml ampoules, cyclizine 50mg/ml ampoules and 7x morphine sulphate 10mg/1ml ampoules. You take the medication bag from her and sort out the medications. Which of the above would need an appropriate record to be made?

A. Haloperidol
B. Water for injection
C. Glycopyronium
D. Morphine sulphate
E. Cyclizine 50mg/ml ampoules

91. Following the previous question, now that you have separated the expired controlled drug from the rest of the medication, which of the following information is not needed when making an appropriate entry in the 'destruction register for patient-returned controlled drugs?

A. Date the drug was returned to the pharmacy
B. Signature of the prescriber
C. Name and signature of the person receiving it
D. Drug name, form, and strength
E. Name of the person returning

92. You are making entries in the controlled drugs register for new CD medications that you have received today from the driver as part of your stock. Which of the following combination would require an entry in the register and safe custody?
A. Buprenorphine 20mg patches and Buspirone tablets
B. Morphine 10mg/5ml solution and meptazinol 200mg tablets
C. Oxycodone 5mg capsules and Fentanyl® lozenges
D. Alimemazine 10mg tablets and fexofenadine tablets
E. Phenobarbital 15mg tablets and tramadol 50mg tablets

93. You are carrying out the CD balance today as part of the weekly clinical governance check for your pharmacy. You find oxycodone ampoules, a controlled drug that expired 2 months ago. How would you dispose of this?
A. You must destroy obsolete, expired, and unwanted Schedule 1 and 2 CDs in the presence of an authorised witness.
B. You must destroy obsolete, expired, and unwanted Schedule 1 and 2 CDs in the presence of a CDAO.
C. You must place obsolete, expired, and unwanted Schedule 1 and 2 CDs in a separate controlled drugs cupboard.
D. You must destroy obsolete, expired, and unwanted Schedule 1 and 2 CDs in the presence of a pharmacy colleague.
E. You cannot destroy obsolete, expired, and unwanted Schedule 1 and 2 CDs within a community pharmacy setting.

94. A gentleman has come to your pharmacy. He tells you that he would like to return some medications. Upon going through the bag of medications, you notice that there are buprenorphine 15mg/hr patches and OxyContin® ampoules. Which of the following statement is incorrect, when dealing with such a situation?

A. You may accept CDs returned by patients for safe destruction and onward disposal. This can be from patients' own homes and from care home organisations providing personal care for their residents.

B. Unwanted returned CDs should be denatured in the presence of another member of staff.

C. Community pharmacies in England can accept waste medicines, including CDs, from sheltered accommodation homes for disposal under the NHS-funded unwanted medicines service.

D. You cannot accept CDs returned by patients for safe destruction and onward disposal. This can be from patients' own homes and from care home organisations providing personal care for their residents.

E. Community pharmacies in England can accept waste medicines, including CDs, from care homes which provide nursing care for disposal under the NHS-funded unwanted medicines service.

95. Miss AZ asks your counter assistant to collect her prescription of two items. The counter assistant finds the pre-dispensed prescription and notices that only 1 of the items is on the shelf in the dispensary. The second item listed on the prescription is in the controlled drugs

cabinet. Which of the following could have been prescribed on this prescription?

A. Diazepam 10mg tablets and gabapentin 300mg capsules
B. Fentanyl® lozenges 1mg tablets and buprenorphine 20mcg/hr patches
C. Temazepam 10mg tablets and clobazam 10mg tablets
D. Pregabalin 75mg capsules and clonazepam 2mg tablets
E. Dihydrocodeine 30mg tablets and morphine sulphate 10mg/5ml oral solution

96. You are the lead pharmacist working on the ambulatory care unit today. You are asked to supply drug XX for a patient urgently. You have supplied the drug against a valid prescription and are now making an entry of the CD supply. Which of the following could drug XX be?

A. Buspirone tablets
B. Buprenorphine patches
C. Methadone oral solution
D. Butec® patches
E. Codeine tablets

97. Miss GT is a new member of staff who joined your team today. She has not got any pharmacy experience before, hence, you allow her to shadow other members of staff as part of the induction. Miss GT notices that another colleague is placing most of the medication stock on the dispensary shelves, however, some medications are kept to one side to be kept safe in the controlled drugs cabinet. Which of the following would be placed in the CD cabinet?

A. Flecainide
B. Flupenthixol
C. Fesoterodine

D. Fentanyl®
E. Fenofibrate

98. A care worker has come in from your local nursing home asking for an emergency supply of medication for Miss TK, a resident. You are presented with the patient's empty box of phenobarbital medication that is used to manager her epilepsy. A 28-day supply was last issued 1 month ago, and the patient has no other medication. The care worker has told you that Miss TK took her last dose last night. Today is a Saturday and she has no more doses of phenobarbital left and is requesting to an emergency supply. Which of the following is the most appropriate action to take?
   A. You cannot issue an emergency supply of a controlled drug; hence you need to refer the patient to an out-of-hours service.
   B. Supply an emergency supply of up to 5 days' worth of treatment for the patient, if appropriate.
   C. Supply an emergency supply of up to 7 days' worth of treatment for the patient, if appropriate.
   D. Supply an emergency supply of up to 28 days' worth of treatment for the patient, if appropriate.
   E. Supply an emergency supply of up to 30 days' worth of treatment for the patient, if appropriate.

99. In the UK the GPhC are the statutory regulator for the pharmacy professions/registered pharmacies in Great Britain. Which of the following established the GPhC?
    A. The National Health Service Act 1946 (amended in 2006) which established the GPhC.
    B. The Medicines Act 1968
    C. The Health Act 1999, as amended by the Health and Social Care Act 2008. Enabled the GPhC to be established via the Pharmacy Order 2010.
    D. The Human Medicines Regulations 2012 is the primary legislation which enabled the GPhC to be established via the Pharmacy Order 2010.
    E. The Pharmacy Regulatory Body Act 1991 is the primary legislation which enabled the GPhC to be established via the Pharmacy Order 2010.

100.   You have been involved in setting up a new community pharmacy and are in the process of applying for a wholesale dealer's licence as the business will also trade medicines on a commercial wholesale basis. Where would you apply for this licence?
    A. GPhC
    B. PSNC
    C. PCN
    D. MHRA
    E. EEA MA

101.   The professional activities of a pharmacist are regulated by which of the following?
A. The PDA
B. The GPhC
C. The RPS
D. The NPA
E. The MHRA

102.   Today you are working on the acute care unit of the hospital as part of your rotation as a junior pharmacist. A patient has volunteered to donate blood at the trust. Upon carrying out a medication history with the patient you realise she is on Isotretinoin. Which of the following is the best course of action for you to take?
A. Document the patient's medical, social and history on her records and advise her to remain hydrated before her transfusion.
B. As the patient takes Isotretinoin, remove her from the hospital premises immediately and write to her GP about this event.
C. Counsel the patient on the process involved with giving blood.
D. As the patient is taking Isotretinoin, she should be advised to avoid donating blood during therapy and for at least 1 month after stopping Isotretinoin.
E. As the patient is taking Isotretinoin, she should be advised to avoid donating blood during therapy and for at least 1 year after stopping Isotretinoin.

Answers

Section 1
Situational Judgment Test Questions

1a) Answer: Option A (Very important)
Explanation
The key problem is that Stanley wants to look at Rinky's written essay 30 minutes before their tutorial group meets, which implies that Stanley might want to copy Rinky's essay. The fact that their tutor asked each student to write their own essay is very important to consider in responding to this situation. It means that Rinky would be potentially allowing Stanley to commit an act of academic misconduct by letting him see, and possibly copy the essay. Hence, option A is the correct answer - very important.

1b) Answer: Option D (Not important at all)
Explanation
This factor is not at all important. If Rinky is concerned that Stanley may copy his coursework, then he should not let Stanley look at his essay.

1c) Answer: Option B (Important)
Explanation
If Stanley has asked to copy Rinky's coursework last year also, this strongly suggests that is more likely to copy Rinky's essay rather than just looking at it. The factor is important to consider, as it suggests a pattern of poor behaviour by Stanley that Rinky may want to address in his response. However, this factor is not of the highest importance, since it provides extra information that is useful but not essential in addressing the key problem in the current scenario.

2a) Answer: Option A (very important)
Explanation
The key issue in the scenario is that the patient has confided in the pharmacy student about his weight loss pills and was embarrassed to tell the doctors, who are struggling as a wider MDT to identify the cause of his serious health problems. Nonetheless, if the weight loss capsules can explain the health problems, it is important for Sangeeta to encourage Mr White to inform the doctors. Therefore, the fact that the doctors don't know Mr White has been taking the weight loss capsules is very important for Sangeeta to consider in responding to the patient.

2b) Answer: Option C (Of minor importance)
Explanation
The fact that Sangeeta does not know the exact ingredients that make up the weight loss pills can be classed as minor importance. Since she is a pharmacy student, Sangeeta does not hold the responsibility to diagnose/prescribe treatment to the patient or advise him – or the doctors on the exact ingredients in the weight loss pills. Simply being aware of the weight loss capsules is sufficient for Sangeeta to advise Mr White to disclose the information to the doctors/nurses. This could then help them to investigate the constituents of those capsules. This issue is tangential to the key problem in the scenario, and to Sangeeta's potential response, so it is of minor importance.

2c) Answer: Option A (Very important)
Explanation
This factor is of the utmost importance. It gives Sangeeta a reason to suggest to Mr White that he tell the doctors about the weight loss capsules. She could offer to help him speak to the doctors.

2d) Answer: Option B (Important)
Explanation

This factor is important since it links with the patient's personal; perceptive feelings and explains why Mr White hasn't already told the doctors about the weight loss capsules. Sangeeta should bear this factor in mind when encouraging the patient to speak to the doctors, as he may still be reluctant to do so. She should not make him feel bad or guilty about being embarrassed, for example. But this factor is not of the highest importance since the main problem is that the weight loss capsules are a likely explanation for Mr White's health problems. The fact that the patient feels embarrassed is still significant, but it is subordinate to the main problem. Thus, this factor is important but not of the greatest importance.

3a) Answer: Option B (Important)
Explanation

The key problem is that the trainee pharmacist has a new patient that he used to know socially. This factor is important to consider, as it suggests that the trainee pharmacist and patient do not currently have a close personal relationship, since Jonathan has not seen the patient socially in the last few years. Thus, it is probably not an ethical issue for Jonathan to treat this patient. However, note that this factor is not of the highest importance since Jonathan will still need the patient to consent to being treated by a social acquaintance. But this factor makes it more likely that the patient would want to consent to be treated by Jonathan, so it is important to consider in responding to this situation.

3b. Answer: Option D (Not important at all)
Explanation

This factor is not at all important. The fact that the patient does not seem to recall having met the trainee pharmacist, even after being introduced to him, does not make it acceptable for Jonathan to treat the patient without first obtaining consent. There is strict ethical guidance against healthcare professionals treating patients with whom they have a close personal relationship, and the trainee pharmacist will want to ensure the patient is comfortable being seen to by her before beginning the consultation. It would be wrong to assume the patient will agree without giving the patient the chance to consent, which is of utmost concern for Jonathan.

3c. Answer: Option A (Very important)
Explanation
This factor is very important to consider, as it underlines the need to treat the patient urgently.

3d. Answer: Option A (Very important)
Explanation
This factor is of the highest importance, as it indicates that the patient can give consent to treatment. It will allow the trainee pharmacist to clarify that he has previously known the patient socially, which will help the patient to give informed consent to being treated by Jonathan.

4a. Answer: Option C (Of minor importance)
Explanation
The key problem in the scenario is that the patient, Edith, had a poor-quality night's sleep in the hospital the previous night and would prefer to sleep in her own bed tonight. However, the doctor has told Edith she must stay overnight for observation.
The fact that Edith is not one of the patients that Reeta has been assigned to interview is of minor importance. Reeta will still need to respond to Edith or arrange for one of the doctors to speak with her, even if she isn't one of his assigned patients. Reeta should bear in mind that she does not know anything about Edith's case other than what she has just told him, so the fact that she is not one of her patients is of minor importance.

4b. Answer: Option A (Very important)
Explanation

This factor is essential to consider in responding to the situation in the scenario. Since the doctor has told Edith she should stay in the hospital overnight for observation, it is very important for Reeta to bear this in mind when she responds to Edith. Edith's health could be compromised if she were to leave the hospital instead of remaining overnight for observation.

4c. Answer: Option B (Important)
Explanation

This factor is important to consider. There could be ways of aiding Edith in getting a better night's sleep in the hospital tonight. For example, perhaps she could be provided with earplugs or moved to a quieter part of the ward. However, this factor is not of the highest importance for two reasons. First, the doctor has said Edith should stay overnight in the hospital for observation, so this is necessary whether she can be aided in getting a better night's sleep. Second, Reeta is not responsible for helping Edith get a better night's sleep, though he could potentially raise her concerns with an appropriate member of staff. Thus, this factor is important but not of the highest importance.

5a. Answer: Option A (Very Important)
Explanation

The key problem is that the nurses have started treating Lynne differently after she is featured in the hospital newsletter. Lynne will need to improve her working relationship with the nurses on the ward, which makes sense as she is new to the ward. This factor is very important to consider.

5b. Answer: Option D (Not important at all)
Explanation

This factor is not at all important. As part of a multidisciplinary team, doctors, pharmacists, nurses, and other healthcare professionals must work together to ensure patient safety and quality of care. If Lynne tries to avoid the nurses for the rest of the day, patient safety and quality of care would suffer. A failure to collaborate with the nurses is something that Lynne should therefore not consider.

5c. Answer: Option C (Of minor importance)
Explanation

It is ambiguous if the nurses are laughing and being strange towards Lynne because they just found out she is a lesbian, or if it is simply because of the coverage itself – maybe they think she is a bit full of herself as a hospital 'celebrity' of sorts. It's certainly possible that the nurses are being homophobic towards Lynne, so it's not a terrible idea to raise the matter with the senior nurse on the ward. However, it is a bit premature to do so before trying to speak to the nurses involved, which would be a more direct and local solution. Thus, this factor is of minor importance.

6A. Answer: Option D (Not important at all)
Explanation

The key problem is that Ronny's hair is untidy and dishevelled and her clothes are soaked, yet she is due to attend ward rounds which are about to start. However, she would violate the hospital's strict dress code by allowing patients to see her in her current state. Thus, it is essential that she quickly fixes her hair and changes her clothes. The fact that the consultant leading the ward rounds will be displeased if she is late is entirely unimportant. If Ronny is quick about it, she might still be able to join the ward rounds before they start or be just a little late. But the fact that the consultant would be displeased if she is late would not justify turning up to the ward rounds in her current state.

6b. Answer: Option A (Very important)
Explanation
This factor is very important to consider, as it would make it easy for Ronny to change into scrubs before joining the ward rounds.

6c. Answer: Option B (Important)
Explanation
This factor is important to consider, as Ronny will need to allow a few minutes to tidy her hair. However, this factor is not of the highest importance, as it does not alter Ronny's response to the situation – she will have to fix her hair before joining the ward rounds.

6d. Answer: Option A (Very Important)
Explanation
This factor is also very important, as it provides another solution to the problem of Ronny's-soaked clothes. If she has an extra set of smart clothes in her hospital locker, she will be able to change out of the wet clothes more quickly.

7a. Answer Option A (Very important)
Explanation
The most important factor here is the hospital policy, which offers clear guidance for this situation. Thus, the hospital policy is very important for Seema to consider when responding to the situation.

7b. Answer Option B (Important)
Explanation
This factor would impact Seema's tone and approach to both the patient and his daughter. Seema should also mention the fact that the patient is distressed about being separated from his daughter to the nursing staff in charge in case they are able to consider alternatives. Thus, this factor is important to consider. However, this factor does not ultimately change the fact that the relative cannot accompany the patient in hospital transport, so it is not of the highest importance.

8a. Answer: Option B (Not important)
Explanation
Statement 1 is not important – The free masks from the supply at the hospital entrance are limited to one per person per day. Thus, it would be wrong for John to take extra masks for any reason. His father's financial difficulties are unfortunate, and it's understandable that John may want to support his father. But this factor does not justify breaking the rule about one mask per person per day. The factor is not important to consider.

8b. Answer: Option B (Not important)
Explanation
Statement 2 is not important – The fact that other colleagues have broken a rule does not justify John breaking the rule. This factor is not important, and John would be wrong to consider it in responding to the situation in the scenario.

8c. Answer: Option A (Important)
Explanation
Statement 3 is important – The hospital provides free masks because they are required for staff and visitors to wear to reduce the spread of transmissible infections. If John takes several masks from the supply at the hospital entrance, his actions could result in a shortage of masks, which could in turn result in the increased spread of infections. This would place patients at risk. This is therefore a very important factor that John should consider.

9a. Answer: Option A (Appropriate)
Explanation
Statement 1 is appropriate – The key problem in this scenario is that Pooja is being asked to perform a clinical task that she is not competent in. Since Pooja has not trained in taking blood and has not even practised this task on a dummy, it would be extremely risky for her to take blood from this patient. However,

the problem is complicated by the fact that the GP may not be aware that Pooja has not trained or practised in this clinical task. Thus, the GP's potential annoyance may be based on a misunderstanding of Pooja's level of clinical training. For this reason, it would be appropriate for Pooja to explain she has not practised taking blood before and would not feel comfortable doing so. This response respects the patient's dignity and safety while ensuring that Pooja behaves responsibly and within her level of clinical experience.

9b. Answer: Option B (Inappropriate)
Explanation
Statement 2 is inappropriate – Pooja would put the patient in danger by agreeing to take their blood, as she has never practised this clinical skill. Even if the GP is in the room guiding her step by step, Pooja should not put the patient in this position in the first place. Proceeding with taking the patient's blood implies that Pooja is competent to do so when she knows she is not. Furthermore, the chances of a complication occurring are high as she has not developed the required clinical skill. This response is thus not appropriate.

9c. Answer: Option B (Inappropriate)
Explanation
Statement 3 is inappropriate – This response may seem acceptable at first glance but note that it involves Pooja promising the GP to take blood from the next patient after observing the process with the current patient. This means that Pooja has not clarified her lack of practice or training in this essential clinical skill. It also means she will likely not be significantly better prepared after observing the GP take blood from the current patient. The next patient could require blood to be taken later the same day, so this merely defers the issue without addressing it sufficiently. It is not an appropriate response.

10a. Answer: Option A (A very appropriate thing to do)
Explanation

The key problem for Jack is that the patient wants to pray her illness away, but Jack is not religious and is an atheist, therefore, is not comfortable joining in the prayer. There is obviously a further problem for the patient, who appears to be struggling with her very recent terminal diagnosis. Offering the opportunity for the patient to discuss her concerns about her illness with someone is therefore very appropriate. It deflects from the requested prayer and allows the patient to address any concerns in a direct, helpful manner.

10b. Answer: Option D (A very inappropriate thing to do)
Explanation

Whilst this response is factually true, it is not a helpful response to the patient's stressful situation. It's also not right for healthcare professionals/students to share their religious beliefs with patients, as they are expected to respect each patient's right to their own beliefs. This response is thus extremely inappropriate.

10c. Answer: Option A (A very appropriate thing to do)
Explanation

This response deflects from the awkward situation, allowing Jack to suggest a more helpful approach that is likely to help address the patient's concerns about her diagnosis. This response is highly appropriate.

10d. Answer: Option C (Inappropriate but not awful)
Explanation

This response is not awful since it is an attempt to refocus on the task at hand. However, it is not a good response, since it entirely avoids the patient's concerns about her diagnosis. The response is therefore inappropriate, but not awful.

11a. Answer: Option B (Appropriate but not ideal)
Explanation

The key problem is that Dr Ralph can see Joshua's login username and password for the patient records database on the cover of his notebook. This means that anyone could see the login details, which could compromise the confidentiality of patient records. Thus, it is appropriate for Dr Ralph to initiate a discussion about the confidentiality of these records. However, this response is not ideal, because it is extremely indirect. An ideal response would directly address the key problem with Joshua, allowing him to address the doctor's concerns immediately.

11b. Answer: Option C (Inappropriate but not awful)
Explanation

This is not an awful thing for Dr Ralph to say, but neither is it appropriate. Whilst this would technically secure Joshua's login details for the current shift, the login details would be exposed again as soon as he removes his notebook from his locker. Thus, as a temporary solution, the response is not awful, but it is inappropriate as it fails to address the issue in a way that would lead to a more constructive, permanent solution.

11c. Answer: Option A (A very appropriate thing to do)
Explanation

This is a very appropriate thing to say. It would initiate a discussion of what Dr Ralph has observed, ensuring that Joshua has a chance to resolve the problem and maintain the confidentiality of patient records. It is an ideal response.

11d. Answer: Option A (A very appropriate thing to do)
Explanation

This response is also extremely appropriate. As Joshua's supervisor, it is perfectly acceptable for Dr

Ralph to instruct him to remove the login details from the notebook and ensure that they are destroyed. This is a direct, local solution that would resolve the key problem in the scenario, so it is ideal. Note that there is no distinction between the final two responses, in that both are ideal responses to the scenario. Do not be put off by responses that seem different in tone – the fact that the third response is a gentler question and the fourth is a more forceful command does not alter the fact that each, on its own, is an ideal response. Each of these options is ideal because it is a direct, local solution to the key problem.

12a. Answer: Option D (A very inappropriate thing to do)
Explanation
There are two key problems in this scenario: first, Amir does not want to attend a compulsory fire safety training that is required for their upcoming work in the pharmacy; second, Amir asks Sanjay to sign his name for him on the sign-in sheet. An ideal response will address one or both problems. Whilst this response might appear to do so, it is awful, since it leaves open the possibility of Amir leaving the training after the first ten minutes. Suggesting that it is acceptable to avoid compulsory training, in whole or part, is extremely inappropriate.

12b. Answer: Option A (A very appropriate thing to do)
Explanation
This response is very appropriate, as it gives a good reason for Amir to attend the training. Note that by encouraging Amir to attend the training, Sanjay can avoid engaging with the request to forge Amir's attendance on the sign-in sheet, which is unnecessary if Amir comes along to the training.

12c. Answer: Option A (A very appropriate thing to do)
Explanation
This response is very appropriate, as it allows Sanjay to decline to sign Amir's name whilst also encouraging him to join the fire safety training.

12d. Answer: Option B (Appropriate but not ideal)
Explanation
This response is not inappropriate, as it is the best course of action if Amir decides not to attend the training. Their tutor will have to be notified, and it is likely that Amir will have to make up the training or potentially delay his work at the pharmacy. However, the response is not ideal, as ideally, Sanjay should encourage Amir to join the fire safety training.

13a. Answer: Option B (Appropriate but not ideal)
Explanation
There are two key problems in this scenario. First, and more urgent, is the patient's query about 'whether he really needs the operation'. Second, and potentially compounding the first problem, is the fact that the patient has mistaken a student for a doctor. Whilst it is important that Claire not imply that she is a doctor – she should not give the patient medical advice, for example – the patient's anxiety about the impending surgery is the more pressing issue here. This response addresses the second problem while overlooking the first. There is nothing wrong with Claire apologising and explaining that she is a pharmacy student, so the response is not inappropriate. However, the response fails to engage with the patient's concerns about the upcoming operation, so it is not an ideal response.

13b. Answer: Option D (A very inappropriate thing to do)

Explanation

The patient has raised his concerns with Claire, who is wearing scrubs and a hospital name badge. Whilst it is true Claire is not a doctor, she clearly works at the hospital, so it is wrong for her to tell the patient to raise his concerns with one of the doctors during the next ward rounds – which might not occur for some time. Claire would handle the situation more professionally by offering to speak to one of the doctors, or by asking one of the doctors to come and speak to the patient.

14a. Answer: Option A (A very appropriate thing to do)

Explanation

The patient is causing a significant ethical issue for the consultant by giving her money in an apparent request to move up the list for an organ transplant. There's also a legal issue since it is illegal to pay for organ donation in the United Kingdom. Thus, Linda must return the money to the patient, and it would also be advisable to explain the ethical problems caused by such an offer. This response is therefore extremely appropriate.

14b. Answer: Option D (A very inappropriate thing to do)

Explanation

This response is not at all appropriate, as a healthcare professional she should not threaten a patient in this manner. There are much better ways for Linda to deal with this situation without resorting to such threats. For example, Linda could explain the ethical and legal problems involved in the patient's behaviour.

14c. Answer: Option C (Inappropriate but not awful)

Explanation

It does seem that the patient has made repeated attempts to offer Linda inducements to move her up the transplant list, so it is understandable that she might wish to remove herself from involvement in her care. The patient's behaviour is bad, so it is not awful for Linda to respond in this manner. However, this response is not appropriate for a couple of reasons. First, it fails to explain the problems involved in this behaviour to the patient; Linda would do better to raise her concerns directly with the patient. Second, this response would have a high likelihood of leaving one of Linda's colleagues in the same situation with this patient, who would presumably continue to offer inducements to the new doctor. Thus, Linda should seek a more direct, local solution with this patient. As a result, this response is inappropriate, but not awful.

15a. Answer: Option A (A very appropriate thing to do)
Explanation
The key problem is that Arjun has never carried out this clinical activity and taken blood from a patient and feels nervous about doing so without supervision. However, at the same time, the department is very busy, so he has not met the doctor supervising his placement. It would be very appropriate for Arjun to insist on being supervised when he takes blood from the patient. It would also be very appropriate for Arjun to ask to speak to the supervising doctor before drawing the blood, which would allow Arjun to share his concerns and ask to be supervised.

15b. Answer: Option A (A very appropriate thing to do)
Explanation
This response addresses the key problem directly. It is therefore highly appropriate.

15c. Answer: Option D (A very inappropriate thing to do)
Explanation
This response may seem appropriate, given Arjun's nervousness and inexperience. However, note that this

response does not involve Arjun mentioning those facts to the nurse. Instead, it's a blanket refusal to draw blood from the patient, which could easily be misinterpreted. This response is very inappropriate.

16a. Answer: Option D (A very inappropriate thing to do)
Explanation

The key problem is that the patient uses a wheelchair but cannot enter the GP surgery due to scaffolding blocking the wheelchair ramp. The fact that Nelly is running late for her placement is not especially important – the patient is having trouble, so she should prioritise helping the patient. This response is very inappropriate, as it could seem dismissive to the patient. It is also quite unspecific as to exactly whom Nelly would be sent to help the patient – there is no way for the patient to follow up if help does not arrive.

16b. Answer: Option A (A very appropriate thing to do)
Explanation

It is always very appropriate to apologise to a patient when something has gone wrong. Note that this applies even if the apology is only an aspect of the response.

16c. Answer: Option C (Inappropriate but not awful)
Explanation

This response is somewhat on the fence, it is part good and part bad. It is good for Nelly to offer to find someone to help but asking the patient if he minds waiting is not good – the patient has no way of entering the building, so it is quite strange to ask him if he minds waiting as he has no choice in the matter. Thus, the response is inappropriate, but not awful. Note that this response could be ideal if the first part was framed differently – for example, if Nelly had explained to the patient there would be a short wait while she finds someone to help.

17a. Answer: Option A (A very appropriate thing to do)
Explanation
There are two problems in this scenario. The key problem is that Ricky's portion of the group work is full of grammatical errors and incorrect claims about the published research on their topic. This main problem is compounded by a secondary problem, which is that the other group members have given a very terse, unhelpful reply ('it's good') which could lead to no further action to correct or improve Ricky's work. Yet Nikita feels that further action is necessary, so she must do something to address her concerns. Suggesting that some group members proofread the group's work before submitting the final report would help to address these concerns, and it is a solution that avoids putting blame on Ricky or spending time on the specific problems in his work. It is an ideal response.

17b. Answer: Option B (Appropriate but not ideal)
Explanation
There is nothing particularly wrong in asking the other group members to give more specific comments to Ricky, so this response is not inappropriate. However, it is not ideal, because Nikita is pressing the other group members to voice her concerns. If Nikita feels that there are issues in Ricky's work that need to be addressed, then she would do better to voice the concerns herself or find a constructive way of addressing them.

17c. Answer: Option D (A very inappropriate thing to do)
Explanation
This response is extremely inappropriate since it is not a constructive approach to the problems in Ricky's work or to the other group members' lack of engagement. It would be far better for Nikita to respond in a way that is more sensitive and subtle to the challenges that the group is facing.

18a. Answer: Option A (A very appropriate thing to do)
Explanation

The key problem is that the junior pharmacist is behaving very strangely. Since the lead pharmacist was told about similar behaviour the day before, it appears to be an ongoing problem that will need to be addressed as a matter of urgency. It is unclear why the junior pharmacist is behaving this way – it could be caused by stress, or it could be a sign of some larger problem, such as drug or alcohol abuse, or mental health issues. Asking the junior pharmacist how he is getting on with his work is a good way of initiating a discussion since it would allow the junior pharmacist to address any concerns with his work; for example, if he is feeling stressed now. It would also give the lead pharmacist an opening for raising concerns about the junior pharmacist's behaviour. This response is therefore extremely appropriate.

18b. Answer: Option D (A very inappropriate thing to do)
Explanation

This response is entirely inappropriate. Since the lead pharmacist was told about the junior pharmacist's behaviour the day before and the current behaviour is far worse than perceived, there is no reason to wait before addressing it. Most worryingly, waiting to address the behaviour would allow the junior pharmacist to see patients in his current condition, which could lead to negative consequences for patient safety and care, or to public confidence in the profession.

18c. Answer: Option B (Appropriate but not ideal)
Explanation

There is nothing wrong with making a note of the junior pharmacist's behaviour. The lead pharmacist may well need to keep a record of this in case further action is necessary. However, this response does not directly address the behaviour, so it is appropriate, but not ideal.

19a. Answer: Option A (A very appropriate thing to do)
Explanation
The key problem is that Lauren has been given tasks that do not relate to the purpose of her attachment. It would be extremely appropriate for Lauren to email the academic tutor supervising the attachment to share her concerns. This tutor is responsible for ensuring that the placement goes well, so they would be well-positioned to support Lauren.

19b. Answer: Option C (Inappropriate but not awful)
Explanation
This response is not especially appropriate – it suggests that Lauren does not feel strongly enough about her education to stand up for herself, so it's inappropriate, but not awful. Whilst the response is bad for Lauren's learning, there are no negative consequences for patients, the profession more broadly, or professional relationships – so there is nothing that makes it a (D) rather than a (C).

19c. Answer: Option A (A very appropriate thing to do)
Explanation
This response is a direct, local solution to the key problem in this scenario, so it is very appropriate. It would have a good chance of addressing her concerns, and it is a very responsible and professional thing for Lauren to do in these circumstances.

20a. Answer: Option C (Inappropriate but not awful)
Explanation
This would come across as rather impertinent of Penny, so it is not an appropriate response. However, the response is not awful because Penny has a point about the pharmacist's views, which are not evidence-

based, impacting patients and potentially discouraging patients from taking the vaccine.

20b. Answer: Option A (A very appropriate thing to do)
Explanation
This would be very appropriate as it might allow the pharmacist to reflect on whether there is evidence supporting his belief in a non-confrontational manner.

21a. Answer: Option A (A very appropriate thing to do)
Explanation
This would be very appropriate. Students should prioritise attending to their own well-being, so the GP appointment should take place without further delay. The tutor should be sympathetic and accommodating to this request since it concerns the student's well-being.

21b. Answer: Option D (A very inappropriate thing to do)
Explanation
This would be inappropriate since Sheetal should be allowed to attend to her own welfare and has already rescheduled the appointment twice. It would be unreasonable for Sheetal to have to wait two more weeks for the GP appointment due to his tutor's request.

22a. Correct option is most appropriate
22b. Correct option is least appropriate
Explanation
Since the project has been set as a joint project by the university tutor, and both Syon and Jamal will be assessed on the project, they both must contribute to the project equally. Therefore, the least appropriate action Syon could take is to work alone to complete the research, seeing as this represents most of the work on the project and all the research must be completed in the next two weeks. If Syon took this action, it would

make her responsible for most of the joint project, violating the fundamental rule about equal contribution to group work. It would not be good to ask the university tutor to extend the deadline due to Jamal's sporting commitments, but this response isn't as bad as Syon doing all the research herself since it would potentially allow the students to divide the research equally. The ideal response is to encourage Jamal to find a way to contribute equally to the project. He should be able to find an alternative arrangement allowing him to complete coursework alongside his preparations for the sporting event.

23a) Correct option is most appropriate
23b) Correct option is least appropriate
Explanation
The key problem is that one pharmacy student has implied that the patient's new medication gives 'every reason to be optimistic' even though the patient's condition is terminal, with the new medication only improving their quality of life rather than treating or curing his underlying condition. It is understandable that a pharmacy student might feel uncomfortable addressing patient concerns relating to mortality, but this sort of issue will come up in medical practice, so students must learn to give honest, direct advice to patients without misleading them or giving them false hope.

Since Carmen has already made the comments, Gerry would best make clear that the new medication cannot cure the patient's condition, though it should improve his quality of life. This is an ideal response, so it is the most appropriate option.
Note that there is nothing wrong with asking the patient if he has questions about his prognosis that they could share with one of the doctors, so this response is appropriate. However, it is not ideal since it fails to

acknowledge or deal with Carmen's misleading comments.

Gerry must not do anything that would make the situation worse. Telling the patient that Carmen's comments are misleading and that he should not have false hope may seem superficially appealing, but this is an incredibly harsh, almost cruel, response. The scenario suggests the patient feels relieved by Carmen's comments, implying that the patient has been misled. But there are far better ways of clarifying the situation and allowing the patient to retain some sense of dignity. Furthermore, the fact that Carmen has made misleading comments is not the patient's problem – it's the impact of these comments on the patient that must be addressed directly with the patient. Gerry could potentially discuss the misleading nature of Carmen's comments with her outside the presence of the patient, or in discussion with the consultant, but it would be unprofessional to criticise Carmen's professionalism to the patient.

24A) Correct option is most appropriate
24B) Correct option is least appropriate
Explanation
The key problem in this question is that Michael seems to be working poorly on the ward. If Michael is forgetting to perform tasks, this could put patients at risk. Sarah has a duty not to be negligent to any factors putting patients at risk, so she should call Michael out on his behaviour.

The **most appropriate** course of action is to ask Michael whether any factors impact his ability to work. Sarah does not know of Michael's personal life, which could be impacting Michael's ability to work. Although healthcare professionals should be able to leave their personal life behind them whilst working, there will be times when this is not possible, in which case the professional should recognise their limits and leave work for a while. In this case, Michael perhaps needs some help to realise that he is not coping well – Sarah could help him determine if this is the case by speaking to him.

The **least appropriate** course of action is to keep a written record of the times when Michael arrives late or leaves early. This does not solve the key problem and would allow it to continue, with potentially devastating consequences for patient health and safety. Sarah already has enough information about Michael's poor working habits, along with his tendency to arrive late and leave early, that she would be justified in escalating the situation to a supervisor after first attempting a direct, local solution by raising the matter with Michael. There is no need to wait and gather evidence, delaying the steps required to change or improve Michael's behaviour.

Warning Michael that he needs to focus on his work more may seem acceptable at first glance since it attempts to solve the key issue, which is the fact that Michael is not performing well at work. However, Sarah should try to be empathetic, and remember that she forms a team with Michael. Confronting Michael about his work without trying to understand if there are any factors leading to his poor performance could damage the relationship between Michael and Sarah, especially if Michael takes offence. It would be unprofessional for Sarah to take such an aggressive stance against Michael given that they are both junior pharmacists – she is his peer, rather than his senior or supervisor.

25a. Correct option is most appropriate
25b. Correct option is least appropriate
Explanation
It is unclear whether the dispenser's behaviour with her backpack is a sign of stealing or something else – for example, she might have engaged in a personal activity, such as changing clothes, in the storeroom. Thus, it would be very inappropriate for Monica to inspect the storeroom to try and deduce what the dispenser might have taken. As a pharmacy student, she is not responsible for investigating possible instances of theft. There is nothing wrong with discussing his concerns about potential workplace misconduct at the next meeting of her tutorial group, but this response does not engage at all with the immediate situation and is not an urgent response to the situation that Monica has observed. Instead, Monica should talk to a different member of the pharmacy, ideally the person supervising her placement, about the incident she has seen.

Answers

Section 2
Clinical Pharmacy, Law, and Ethics Questions

1. Answer option B is correct. Children under the age of 13 years are considered too young legally to consent to any type of sexual activity. Unless backed by appropriate evidence and mutually agreed upon, cases such as this must be taken very seriously and perhaps reported to appropriate bodies such as social services.

2. Answer option B is correct as there is no legal limit in selling effervescent paracetamol OTC. Also, no limit to granules, solutions or liquids of paracetamol that can be sold. The legal OTC sale limit of 100x unit sale is for aspirin and paracetamol non-effervescent tablets or capsules.

3. Option A is correct. Due to the risk of addiction, products containing codeine/dihydrocodeine should not be used for longer than 3 days OTC. All the other statements are incorrect as up to 720mg of pseudoephedrine and 180mg of ephedrine can be sold as a pharmacy-only medication without a prescription. Duloxetine is a POM medication, and cannot be sold OCT.

4. Answer option E is correct, the age of the patient is only needed if the patient is aged under 12 years, not 18 years. Hence the wrong option, see below for legal requirements.

7 requirements for any prescription (NHS / Private) to be valid are.
- Signature (signed by the prescriber)
- Address of the prescribing practitioner

- The prescription must have a valid date on it, usually valid up to 6 months from the appropriate date, or 28 days for a schedule 2,3,4 controlled drug.
- Name of the patient
- Address of the patient
- Prescribers' particulars such as name and registration number
- Age of the patient if under the age of 12 years

5. Answer option B is correct. Private prescriptions can be repeatable as many times as stated by the prescriber. E.g., can be dispensed more than once. All the other forms stated cannot be dispensed more than once from the same type of prescription form. Although medications can be put on repeat, each repeat supply would need a new prescription to be issued and signed by the prescriber. But on a private prescription, this is not the case and instead can be dispensed more than once off the same form. This can be for human or veterinary private prescriptions. If a number is not stated on a private prescription, then it may be repeated only once from the same form. FP10 MDA prescriptions are not repeatable, however, a single prescription can request several instalments to be dispensed.

6. Answer option C is correct, this is because morphine 10mg/5ml solution is a schedule 5 CD, therefore, is repeatable on a private prescription, however, schedule 2 and 3 drugs are NOT repeatable,

7. Answer option B is correct, dihydrocodeine tartrate 120 mg tablets are classed as a schedule 5 drug and must be dispensed within 6 months of the issue date stated on the prescription assuming an appropriate clinical requirement for the patient. Option D is incorrect as Dihydrocodeine tartrate 120 mg tablet is a schedule 5 controlled drug. Schedule 5 controlled drug prescriptions can be dispensed within 6 months not 12 months or just 28 days of the issue date legally.

8. Answer options B and C are incorrect, this is because private repeatable prescriptions must be kept for 2 years after the FINAL repeatable supply is made against the prescription, not 2 years from the initial supply. Option A is correct because private prescriptions must be kept as a record for audit purposes for 2 years after the supply.

9. Answer option E is the correct answer, this is because patients who have been released from prison and the prescription states HMP 'Her/His Majesty's Prison' in the address are exempt from prescription charges. Hence, all the other options stated are incorrect.

10. Answer option C is the correct answer, prescriptions issued on an FMed 296 form are military prescriptions. These can only be dispensed in pharmacies covered under the (MOD) Ministry of Defence contract. However, if a non-MOD contracted community pharmacy is in receipt of a military prescription, then this can be dispensed as a private prescription against an appropriate charge.

11. Answer option c is correct, schedule 2 and 3 controlled drugs requested to be dispensed on a MOD FMed 296 form cannot be legally issued as they must be issued on an FP10PCD form. As fentanyl is a schedule 2 drug it cannot be dispensed, and the RX must be returned to the prescriber. All the other options can be dispensed. Option E is also true because codeine is a regular POM drug, hence can be issued on a FMed 296 form.

12. Answer option D is correct. Although option C would be ideal, having both the outer and inner container labelled with the appropriate instructions, nonetheless it is not a legal requirement. Hence, option C is incorrect. Option D is correct, as suggested by the national patient safety agency, the actual container of the medication should be labelled, rather than the outer packaging this can ensure that even if the excess outer packaging is discarded, the actual packaging still has instructions for safe administration. Option E is also incorrect, the patient's date of birth is not a legal requirement on dispensing labels.

13. Answer option C is correct.

14. Answer option D is correct, occupational therapists cannot request POM medications against a signed order.

15. Answer option D is correct. Option A 'potassium bromide' cannot legally be supplied as an emergency supply. Option B is incorrect, as hydrocortisone 1% cream is available to purchase as a 15-gram quantity OTC, it could be sold to a patient OTC. Supplying 100g of it would be rather excessive in an emergency supply scenario. Although naproxen 500mg

tablets can be supplied as an emergency supply, 24 tablets would be excessive to cover an emergency, other OTC anti-inflammatory may be a better option to purchase until a prescription is received. Hence, option C is also incorrect. Option E is incorrect, as any quantity of clobetasone butyrate 0.05% cream over 15g is classed as POM, so it can be supplied as the 15g version via an OTC purchase, instead of an emergency supply. In an emergency, 1 inhaler pack of salbutamol may be supplied subject to it being an appropriate supply.

16. Option A is the correct answer, this is because before making a supply of medication under an emergency supply, the pharmacist must deem the situation to be an emergency and be satisfied that the supply is in the best interest of the patient without causing harm. Option E is incorrect, the statement suggests that 'any CD' must not be given as an emergency supply. This statement is false as you can still give up to 5 days of certain CDs such as phenobarbital, or schedule 4/5 CDs.

17. Answer option C is correct, CPCS is an advanced service.

18. Answer option D is correct, a signed order needs to be retained for 2 years from the date of the supply.

19. Answer option A is the incorrect option because it is not permitted by any regulation to be administered to manage an opioid overdose. It is licensed for alcohol or opioid use disorder. Option B is the correct answer, this is because naloxone is an opioid antagonist used to reverse CNS depression,

especially with opioid overdose. It is allowed to be administered by workers to individuals who may have overdosed and are in an emergency in need of naloxone for life-saving purposes. Within an appropriate drug treatment clinic.

20. Answer option D is correct, the pregnancy prevention program was set up to prevent females who are taking teratogenic medications such as oral retinoids, thalidomide, or valproate to become pregnant as such medications have had a high association with birth defects or stillbirths. Healthcare professionals dealing with such female patients must ensure that the patient has received adequate education, are aware of the possible consequences of pregnancy and is tested for pregnancy before and during treatment.

21. Answer option B is correct, this is because alitretinoin is an oral retinoid. As stated in the product license, this medication is associated with serious congenital malformations, thus pregnancy must be avoided in females taking this medication. All the other counselling points are not imminent and not evidence-based, hence incorrect options.

22. Answer option E is correct, this is because isotretinoin is extremely teratogenic and foetal exposure can lead to lead threatening congenital abnormalities. Under the pregnancy prevention program, pregnancy must be ruled out before treatment, contraceptives must be used during treatment, and any pregnancy should be avoided for at 4 weeks after stopping isotretinoin. If isotretinoin is not dispensed within 7 days of the prescription, then this prescription would be classed as expired after the 7 days, the pharmacist must not risk

issuing this prescription after this period and refer the patient back to the prescriber due to the risk of pregnancy. Prescriptions for male patients do not have this 7-day expiry date on the prescription as advised by the MHRA.

23. Answer option C is correct, this is because valproate-containing medications must not be stopped abruptly, and doses must be appropriately managed by a prescriber and monitored closely while titrating a dose. Stopping the medication suddenly could increase her chances of suffering a seizure again, potentially harming both the parent and her child. She should not also just continue with her valproate treatment without informing the prescriber as this place's risks on her unborn child to develop congenital malformations, hence options D and E are incorrect. The patient needs an urgent review by the prescriber.

24. Answer option B is correct, the emergency supply legislation only applies for human use, not veterinary animal use. Hence legally pharmacists cannot issue a supply without a valid veterinary prescription. Options D and E are pointless, signposting the veterinary surgeon elsewhere is not going to help them, you need them to issue a prescription for you to make a supply.

25. Answer option E is correct, optometrist independent prescribers are not allowed to prescribe any controlled drugs. Their scope of practice must be for treating conditions related to the eyes and the surrounding areas.

26. Answer option C is incorrect as physiotherapist-independent prescribers can only prescribe morphine (for injectable/oral use) for patients. Option B is also incorrect. Option E is incorrect as prescribers require a license to prescribe any form of diamorphine, dipipanone and cocaine in treating addiction, and the scope of prescribing for physiotherapists is very restricted. Option a is correct as they can prescribe fentanyl for transdermal administration, morphine for injection/oral use and oral diazepam, dihydrocodeine, lorazepam, oxycodone, and temazepam for appropriate indications. Hence All of the other options stated are incorrect.

27. Answer option B is correct, the scope of prescribing for podiatrist/chiropodist independent prescribers is very limited. They can only prescribe very few schedules 2-5 controlled drugs for oral use, which include diazepam, dihydrocodeine, lorazepam and temazepam. Hence, option B is correct, and all the other options stated are incorrect. Option E is incorrect, brinzolamide eye drops solution is licensed for ophthalmic use, so it would be out of scope for a podiatrist/chiropodist to prescribe.

28. Answer option E is correct. Option A is incorrect, EEA and Swiss-approved prescribers can only prescribe schedule 4 and 5 controlled drugs, Lisdexamfetamine is a schedule 2 drug, hence they cannot prescribe it. Options B and C are also incorrect as community nurse practitioner prescribers/therapeutic radiographers' independent prescribers cannot prescribe any controlled drugs. Option E is the correct answer, nurse and midwife independent prescribers can prescribe schedule 2-5

controlled drugs except for cocaine, dipipanone and diamorphine.

29. Answer option A is correct, as optometrists are registered with the General Optical Council. All other professions stated are registered with the Health and Care Professions Council, the list also includes dieticians, orthoptists, paramedics, physiotherapists, podiatrists, chiropodists, and radiographers

30. Answer option A is correct.

31. Option B is correct, this is because when a pharmacy supplies POM items against a signed order you should retain that for at least TWO years from the date of supply or alternatively make an entry in the private POM register. All the other options are incorrect. Patient-specific directions must be for an individual named patient, however, signed orders do not need to be patient-specific, so option D is incorrect.

32. Answer option E is correct.
- POM-V medicines can only be prescribed by a veterinary surgeon (vet) and supplied by a vet/pharmacist.
- POM-VPS medicines are prescription-only medicines that can be prescribed and supplied by a vet/pharmacist. A written physical prescription would be needed if the prescriber is not the supplier also of the medication.
- NFA-GSL medicines do not require written prescriptions and can be supplied by a vet/pharmacist.
- AVM-GSL medicines are veterinary medicines that are available for sale OTC.

33. Option A is correct, Small Animal Exemption Schemes allows certain medication to be brought into the market without marketing authorisation. For use in small pet animals.

34. Answer option D is correct, as the statement is false, this is because legally the veterinary prescriber must state their RCVS registration number when prescribing schedule 2 or 3 controlled drugs under the cascade, not required for schedule 4 drugs. All the other options stated are correct statements.

35. Answer option C is correct, when a vet is prescribing a schedule 2 or 3 controlled drugs, they must state 'prescribed for the treatment of an animal or herd under my care'. This statement is not needed for all POM medications, nor needed for schedule 4 or 5 drugs.

36. Answer option C is correct, veterinary prescriptions do not need to be submitted to the relevant NHS Agency, only human private prescriptions for schedule 2 and 3 controlled drugs must be submitted to the agency for processing.

37. Answer option B is correct. Options A and C are incorrect as you cannot prescribe veterinary use medication on an FP10SS or private prescription form. For human-use medication to be lawfully prescribed and supplied on a veterinary prescription for animal use, the veterinary surgeon must state that this medication is being prescribed 'for administration under the cascade'. This cascade is an exemption in the Veterinary Medicines Regulations 2013. It allows the supply of human medication for veterinary use,

where licensed veterinary medicine is not available. Options D and E are also false.

38. Answer option E is correct, the pharmacist's registration number is not needed p, however under the Veterinary Medicines Regulations 2013, the rest is needed.

39. Answer option E is correct, veterinary requisition forms do not need to be submitted, but retained for at least 5 years.

40. Answer option B is correct as the statement is incorrect. Although ulipristal and levonorgestrel can be used more than once in the same cycle. They must not be used together in the same cycle.

41. Answer option B is correct. Option E is not even actual legislation in existence, hence, is the incorrect option. Option B the Health act 2006 brings in the concept of an accountable officer. Accountable officers are responsible for supervising and managing the use of CDs, with appropriate auditing and monitoring. They are required to attend local intelligence network meetings. Produce and submit occurrence reports concerning behaviours.

42. Answer option E is correct. A GP10A form is incorrect as it is used as a requisition form for NHS supplies in Scotland. Option B CDRF form is incorrect as it is used as a private requisition form in Scotland. WP10CDF is used as a requisition form in Wales, hence is incorrect. FP10PCD is a standardised private prescription form, hence not appropriate for a requisition request. Option E is correct as FP10CDF forms are used in England as requisition forms.

43. Answer option E is correct as it is a false statement. Although also stated in option B that doctors and dentists can be provided with schedule 2 or 3 CD medications in an emergency, this would be because a requisition form is provided within 24 hours not 72 hours, hence option B is incorrect. All the other statements are true. The original requisition form once processed should be indelibly marked with the supplying pharmacy's name and address and this form must be submitted to the NHSBSA, however, the NOC recommend keeping a copy of the original requisition form for 2 years as good practice for audit purposes.

44. Answer option B is correct because all the other options stated are opioids used as analgesia during labour. Heroin is another recreational term for diamorphine.

45. Answer option D is correct, all the other options stated are legally required, however, the midwife's registration number is not required on the supply order form.

46. Answer option B is correct as the pharmacist can dispense from those instructions written on the prescription, this is because the total quantity is written in words and figures, the strength and form of the oxycodone are stated and the direction for the patient to follow are clear without any abbreviations. Option A cannot be dispensed as the strength of the morphine tablets is not stated and the abbreviation M/R has not been written in full. Regulations stipulate that on controlled drug prescriptions, abbreviations must not be used. Option C is incorrect as the direction for the

morphine are ambiguous and don't state 'how many' to take daily. Option D is incorrect as the quantity does not match in words and figures. Option E is also the incorrect option and cannot be dispensed against as it contains an ambiguous abbreviation, that should've stated 'immediate release' clearly to make it valid.

47. Answer option E is correct, this 30-day treatment period is a professional recommendation, not a legislative requirement, hence, the prescriber can prescribe longer treatments should they have a justifiable reason for the benefit for the patient.

48. Answer option D is correct as the directions are clear and do not have any ambiguity, hence legally can be accepted as instructions on a controlled drugs prescription.

49. Answer option A is correct as the statement is true. Statement B is incorrect because the instalment does not have to be restricted to just 7 days, it could go beyond the 28-day prescription validity period, as long as the initial supply was made to the patient within 28 days. Option C is incorrect as the initial instalment does can be dispensed within 28 days not 7. Options D and E are also incorrect, as the rest of the instalment can be dispensed, processed, or supplied beyond 28 or 30 days.

50. Answer option C is correct, this is because if a patient has missed 3 days' worth of instalments or more, then this causes the patient to lose tolerance to the drug, hence a supply of an instalment could potentially be an overdose for the patient. Hence, option A is incorrect. In this case, the patient must be referred to the drug clinic/ prescriber to get a new prescription.

Option B is incorrect as there is no reason to be involving the CDAO to report a patient with a missed dose. Any missed instalment should never be handed out to the patient, as this introduces the risk of the patient taking more than one dose and perhaps overdosing. Option E is also not appropriate as it may be classed as negligence from your end for not following it up with the prescriber.

51. Answer option D is correct as it is a false statement. Buprenorphine is a schedule 3 controlled drug requiring safe custody. Hence, is incorrect. All the other statements are true.

52. Answer option A is correct, a T28 exemption is an exemption issued by the environmental agency allowing pharmacies to sort and dispose of CDs. To comply with the 2001 regulations, these CDs must be denatured prior to disposal. All the other options are incorrect, especially option D as it describes, a T20 exemption allows you to treat certain waste at water treatment works to reduce the volume for transport, or to make it easier to handle for waste recovery.

53. Answer option A is correct as the statement is false. The patient returned schedule 2, 3 and 4 (part-1) controlled drugs do not require an authorised witness to destroy them legally, although a witness is preferred. However, when destroying expired, obsolete, unwanted schedules 2, 3, 4 (part 1) controlled drugs do require an authorised witness to be present. All the other statements are correct.

54. Answer option E is correct. Option C is incorrect as Sativex does require record keeping despite being a schedule 4 part-1 CD.

All the other options require records to be updated and entries to be made as they are schedule 2 controlled drugs, except for option E which is not a controlled drug at all. Dexamethasone is a steroid, POM.

55. Answer option A is correct. The date of the prescription is not required as part of the CD entry, for a CD that has been handed out. All the other pieces of information stipulated form part of the minimum that must be stated to for an appropriate CD entry.

56. Answer C is correct. Option A is incorrect, as CD register entries can be handwritten in indelible ink or written on an appropriate computerized platform. They do not just have to be in a computerized form. Option B is also incorrect, as the entry must be ideally as soon as the CD transaction is made, otherwise, must be made by the following day of the transaction. Options D and E are also incorrect, authorized witnesses are not required for every CD entry that is made in the register and entries cannot be altered later. Should a correction be necessary then this must be noted in the footnote/margin of the register with the pharmacist's name, signature, and GPhC registration number with the appropriate date. Option C is the correct answer, all CD entries must be written in chronological order of transactions.

57. Answer option A is correct and is not the best course of action to take. As the paracetamol is still unexpired and fine to use for about 3 months, there is no need to immediately destroy and remove them from stock. All the other options stated are true and are actions which you could take to ensure medication

stock is used appropriately and safely without causing wastage. The MHRA has advised drug manufacturers that have an expiration date stating, 'use by 10/24', then such medication can be used safely until the end of that month, so in this case it can be used up until 31/10/24. However, must not be used from 01/11/24 onwards. Placing short-date stickers will help to identify and use these packets first and rotating stock will allow identification during dispensing more efficiently. As packs of 32x 500mg paracetamol can be Sold OTC as a P-only medication. It would be useful to sell some packets OTC, to prevent wastage.

58. Answer option B is the best option portraying patient-centred care and is the correct option. The phrase introduces the healthcare professional to the patient and sets out an agenda for the consultation. The rest of the phrases do not convey patient-centred care and don't empower patients to make informed decisions or listen to their concerns/views.

59. Answer option A is correct. Patients are usually part of several groups which forms their own culture. Age, gender, ethnicity, sexual orientation, nationality, religion, social class, and profession. E.g., check with the person how they want to be addressed, such as transgender. Having an equality/diversity policy or statement prevents misunderstanding and helps to build trust and faith. Everyone's priorities are different. Asking open questions gives them the opportunity. All the other statements are inappropriate for becoming more culturally informed.

60. Answer option A is correct. A punitive culture has a knock-on effect on the way people feel or behave. The fear of punishment prevents any learning or reporting from happening which then reduces the quality of service and patient safety. The rest of the options listed are incorrect as they describe safety culture. The other options are non-punitive which is what workplaces/teams should have, as it describes an open and free culture where the transparency helps everyone to report, learn and grow. Resultantly, this allows for a fair and improved service to be provided and for patients to benefit.

61. Answer option E is correct. The last option relates to punitive culture and being afraid. Everyone makes mistakes, you cannot guarantee they won't be made again, but learn from them. A culture of candour is vital.

62. Answer option B is correct. NRLS stands for National Reporting and Learning System. from June 2012 an online reporting system for patient safety incidents across England and Wales. For Scotland, NHS board operates its on-reporting base. Helps to review near misses also.

63. Answer option E is correct. Pharmacists have the professional, legal, and moral duty to protect children and adults from abuse. They must work with other authorities to safeguard. Should not attempt to investigate, suspect, or make allegations directly. Option E is the correct answer, as a cough is not a sign of direct abuse. Fractures are (physical abuse). Dirty clothes are a form of general (neglect). A behavioural problem is a form of (emotional abuse). STIs can be a form of (sexual abuse).

64. Option A is correct. This is because under the Sexual Offences Act 2009. It remains to be a criminal offence, for those who are involved in any sort of sexual activity with someone who doesn't give free agreement to it. Furthermore, it is a criminal offence for persons involved in sexual acts such as (sexual intercourse, sexual touching, kissing etc) with anyone under the age of 13 whether the young person agrees or not. This can be on the basis that anyone under 13 years lacks the capacity to give valid consent to any sexual act. Under this act, it is also classed as a criminal offence for anyone who is 16 or older to have any kind of sexual contact with someone aged 13, 14 or 15. Under the terms of the Human Rights Act 1998, it must be noted that young people are entitled to similar levels of privacy as adults. A young person's confidentiality should only be breached where appropriate. Ulipristal acetate must not be taken by persons aged under 13 years OTC. Children under 13 years are legally too young to consent to sexual activity. Report to social services unless backed by sufficient evidence.

65. Answer option E is correct, as parenteral/guardian consent or means of communication is not required as part of the Fraser guidelines. A healthcare professional must not tell the parents or persuade them to tell, as you still have a general duty of confidentiality. The Fraser guidelines apply to the advice and treatment relating to contraception and sexual health of the young patient. However, Gillick competency is often used in a wider context to help assess whether the young patient has the maturity to make their own decisions and to understand the

implications of those decisions. Usually, contraception/treatment can be given under an appropriate PGD, prescription, or licence if the young person meets the Fraser guidelines criteria.

66. Answer option A is correct, this is because regular EHC requests from the same patient could be a sign of sexual abuse. Frontline healthcare providers of EHC must take appropriate action to identify and offer confidential support for such patients. All the other options are least likely to be sexual abuse and more relevant to domestic abuse/neglect.

67. Answer option E is correct. Options A and B are incorrect as the vulnerable adults' wishes are not being taken into consideration, hence breaching Mr JL's trust and confidence. Although a patient may be vulnerable, this does not mean that they do not have the capacity, their wishes and beliefs must also be taken into consideration - should they have the mental capacity to make decisions. Thus, the patient's capacity must first be assessed. Consent must be obtained from a person with capacity before disclosing any confidential information or commencing an investigation.

68. Answer option C is correct. Aiming to deprescribe which is vital when optimizing medicines use in patients, it is not part of the 4 core principles of medicines optimization. The goal of optimizing medications for patients is to help them manage their drug treatment better and take ownership of their medications. This would improve health outcomes and reduce waste.

69. Answer option D is correct, 'The Human Medicines Regulation 2012' consolidates a lot of the Medicines act 1968, but not all of it hence the act remains active.

70. Answer option A is correct, all the other options are not relevant to the question, and hence are false. The Veterinary Medicines Regulations (VMR) 2013 set out the UK controls on veterinary medicines. This regulation covers the manufacture, advertising, marketing, supply, and administration of veterinary medication. Persons involved with these medications must comply with the VMR 2013.

71. Answer option B is correct as the statement is false. GSL medication sale does not require the presence or supervision of a pharmacist as stipulated in the HMR 2012.

72. Answer option A is correct, naproxen 250mg tablets are only available on prescription, although you can buy them over the counter for period pain and menstrual cramps as a pharmacy-only medication. Promazine may sound like promethazine it is very different. Promazine is a first-generation antipsychotic, hence is a POM line. Folic acid 5mg tablets are prescription only, however, can be purchased OTC as 400ug tablets. All the other options stated are POM licensed.

73. Answer option D is correct. Orlistat 60mg capsules are the only strength available to purchase OTC-the-counter as a pharmacy (P) medicine in the UK. This medication was reclassified from POM status and licensed for patients aiming to lose body weight who are clinically obese and aged 18 years or over. The only other valid strength that orlistat is available

as is 120mg tablets which are licensed as POM. All the other strengths stated are non-existent hence invalid answer options.

74. Answer option A is correct. The sale and supply of pseudoephedrine/ephedrine are restricted, as large quantities of pseudoephedrine and ephedrine are the core ingredient to produce methylamphetamine which is an illicit drug widely known as 'Crystal Meth'. Option B is a false statement, this is because a 30mg to 60mg dose of pseudoephedrine is licensed and does not cause hypotensive effects. However, may precipitate hypertensive effects instead due to sympathomimetic activity. It is unlawful to sell or supply any pseudoephedrine product at the same time as an ephedrine product without a prescription (Regulation 237 of Human Medicines).

75. Answer option E is correct, as a patient who makes 'infrequent' requests for drugs; would unlikely be at risk of overdosing/overusing the drug and hence not a sign of abuse. A patient who lacks appropriate symptoms and still requests to purchase a drug or presents with opportunistic/impatient behaviour and rehearsed answers should be dealt with carefully. Suspicions can be reported to the local GPhC inspector or local CD liaison police officer.

76. Answer option C is correct, buprenorphine preparations are classed as schedule 3 drugs and legally require safe custody, kept locked and secure away from regular stock. All the other medications listed are exempt from safe custody. Tramadol is a schedule 4 drug not requiring safe custody.

77. Answer option B is correct, under the Misuse of Drugs Act 1971, instalment prescriptions for Physeptone must be dispensed as directed on the prescription. As the patient missed his dose on the 24th of May and the 25th of May - he can still have his daily dose for the 26th of May, only of 35ml. Patients who miss 3 days or more of their regular prescribed dose of opioid maintenance with Physeptone are at risk of overdose because of loss of tolerance. However, as Mr FG had only missed 2 days' worth of doses, he did not need to be referred to the prescriber.

78. Answer option D is correct, Schedule 2 and 3 controlled drugs prescriptions, such as those for methadone and buprenorphine, are valid for 28 days after the 'appropriate date' on the prescription. The date on which the prescription was signed by the person issuing it known as the (signature date) is when the prescription was signed and is recorded next to the signature box. Legally the date of signing must be stated and controlled drugs prescription under the Misuse of Drugs Act 1971 should be dispensed within 28 days of that signed date.

79. Answer option D is correct, as morphine 10mg/5ml oral solution is classed as a schedule 5 controlled drug, prescriptions for this category are valid to dispense within 6 months of the issue date, any period over the 6-month period from the issue date would deem the prescription as expired.

80. Answer option B is correct, prescriptions for schedule 2 controlled drugs are only valid to dispense and supply for up to 28 days from the issue date. Any period over the 28-day period

from the issue date would deem the prescription as expired.

81. Answer option A is correct, as 'Kaolin and Morphine Mixture BP' is a 'pharmacy only' medication, it can be sold to patients under the supervision of a pharmacist. Hence all the other options stated are incorrect. Issuing the product only with a prescription is incorrect, although it may be supplied in that manner. Under the GPhC standards for pharmacy professionals, you must not lie and work honestly and with integrity, therefore option D is incorrect, lying to the patient is not the best course of action to take.

82. Answer option C is the best course of action to take. Antibiotics are for an acute supply, usually for acute indication. The fact that it has been almost 6 months since this prescription was issued by the prescriber, the antibiotic may no longer be indicated for the patient. On the flip side, the prescription may be suitable for the patient and the prescriber may have advised using it for acute infections at a later stage, or as a rescue pack perhaps. Thus, refusing the supply or dispensing the antibiotic without querying it further would be inappropriate action by the pharmacist.

83. Answer option E is correct, all schedule 2 and 3 drug prescriptions must have the total quantity written in words and figures for the prescription to be legally valid. The rest of the options stated are incorrect as they do not invalidate the prescription and instead allow for it to be dispensed.

84. Answer option B is correct and the best answer in this scenario, as venlafaxine is licensed as a POM in the UK, you cannot sell it OTC, however, you can signpost him to a prescriber to assess his situation and perhaps get it prescribed. You should not give him an emergency supply, this can be for several reasons such as not knowing the dose, strength, or formulation. Also, the patient has not been able to produce any evidence and you do not have any records to make an informed decision against, thus the supply could, in fact, be detrimental to the patient. Telling the patient to go back to Brazil is not helping him and could be perceived as a form of neglect from yourself. Selling the patient diphenhydramine wouldn't be ideal as it cannot be used as a substitute for venlafaxine.

85. Answer option D is correct. As per the Human Medicines Regulations 2012, the patient's signature is not a legal requirement for an NHS prescription. However, all the other options stated are needed for the prescription to be legally valid. If any of them is missing, then you should not dispense and get the prescription amended by the prescriber.

86. Answer option D is correct. The OTC license for chlorphenamine does not allow it to be sold for veterinary use, hence making the supply would be off license use and this is not permitted with OTC sales. You cannot make an emergency supply for animals, although not OTC, the supply could be made against a valid prescription for Miss PV's dog from the vet. Just because the medicine was recommended by a prescribing practitioner does not mean it has to be supplied. You as the pharmacist must exercise your professional judgment.

87. Answer option B is correct. Cinnarizine 15mg tablets are licensed as a pharmacy-only medication, therefore these can be sold OTC under the appropriate supervision of a pharmacist. Mr SD needs the medication urgently, although you can refer him to the out-of-hours service to get a prescription, this may take some hours. Thus, he would have missed his dose and perhaps suffer from vertigo because of the failure to supply, so option C is not the best course of action. Under the Human Medicines Regulations 2012, pharmacists are allowed to make an emergency supply, however as cinnarizine can be purchased over the counter, then that must be considered first.

88. Answer option B is correct, Buccolam® is the only drug stated that is a prescription-only medication. All the other options stated are available to purchase OTC for appropriate indications. Buccolam® is an Oro-mucosal form of midazolam (benzodiazepine) used to treat seizures. As you are told that the customer's mother purchased it before OTC, she could not have purchased midazolam without a prescription.

89. Answer option A is correct. Dexamphetamine is a schedule 2 controlled drug. It must be kept under safe custody in a controlled drug unit. All the other drugs are standard non-CD POM medications which can be stocked away with normal stock.

90. Answer option D is correct, morphine sulphate 10mg/1ml ampoules are classed as a schedule 2 controlled drug. All the other drugs are standard non-CD POM medications which can be stocked away with normal expired stock.

91. Answer option B is correct, the prescriber who issued the medication does not need to sign the entry made on the patient returns controlled drugs register. However, all the other pieces of information are necessary when making an entry for audit purposes.

92. Answer option C is correct, both oxycodone and fentanyl are schedule 2 controlled drugs, thus, requiring entries to be made in the CD registers as well as safe custody. Buprenorphine is a schedule 3 controlled drug requiring safe custody, but no entries need to be kept, thus, option A is incorrect. Phenobarbital and tramadol are schedule 4 controlled drugs not requiring safe custody or entry.

93. Answer option A is correct. It is a legal requirement under the 2001 regulations for pharmacy contractors to have stocks of obsolete, expired, and unwanted Schedule 1 and 2 CDs destroyed in the presence of an authorised witness, they do not have to be a colleague from the pharmacy.

94. Answer option D is correct. Pharmacies can accept CDs returned by patients for safe destruction and onward disposal. This can be from patients' homes and care home organisations providing personal care for their residents. When handling unwanted Schedule 2, Schedule 3 and Schedule 4 (part 1) CDs returned from patients' homes/care homes providing personal care, you should place these into waste containers only after the CD has been rendered irretrievable (i.e., by denaturing). Community pharmacies in England can accept waste medicines, including

CDs, from care homes which provide nursing care for disposal under the NHS funded unwanted medicines service.

95. Answer option C is correct. Option A is incorrect, both diazepam and gabapentin do not require safe custody. Option B is also incorrect as both fentanyl® and buprenorphine would be kept inside the CD cabinet. However, in the scenario, it stated that 1 item was found pre-dispensed on the shelf and only 1 other item was in the cabinet. Option C is correct because temazepam requires safe custody while clobazam does not, hence fits in with the scenario. Both options D and E are incorrect, this is because the medications listed do not require safe custody, and thus cannot be the ones listed in the scenario.

96. Answer option C is correct, as methadone is a schedule 2 controlled drug, an appropriate entry is required to be made in the CD register when a supply is made to ensure an accurate balance is maintained. All the other drugs do not require a CD entry to be made.

97. Answer option D is correct as it is the only schedule 2 CD listed from the list that requires safe custody. The rest of the drugs can be placed along with the regular pharmacy-dispensary stock.

98. Answer option B is correct, when issuing emergency supplies, no greater quantity shall be supplied than to provide 5 days' worth of treatment for a patient in an appropriate emergency.

99. Answer option C is correct. The Health and Social Care Act 2008 Act gave the GPhC the function to be the pharmacy regulator. Under this, the Pharmacy Order 2010 formed the GPhC as an independent statutory regulator, with the responsibility to maintain pharmacy, pharmacist, and technician registration records.

100. Answer option D is correct. A wholesaler dealer's license / wholesale authorisation for a pharmacy must be applied from the MHRA. This license must be granted before the pharmacy business can sell or supply medicines to anyone other than the patient using the medicine. A wholesaler licence is also known as a wholesale dealer licence or wholesale distribution authorisation.

101. Answer option B is correct. The pharmacist's defence association provide a range of defence services and provide professional indemnity insurance for pharmacists. The GPhC regulate pharmacists' activity/registration. The Royal Pharmaceutical council are the professional leadership body for pharmacists. The national pharmacy association provide protection and indemnity cover for pharmacists/technicians. The Medicines and Healthcare products Regulatory Agency regulates medicines, and medical devices in the UK. While being a pharmacist in the UK, pharmacists must comply with the GPhC standards for pharmacy professionals.

102. Answer option D is correct, this is because the metabolites of Isotretinoin may remain in the donor's blood, hence may pose a potential risk to the recipient receiving the blood if they are pregnant, as it would harm the baby.

Printed in Great Britain
by Amazon

50619261R00106